THE SIREN AND THE SEASHELL

THE TEXAS PAN AMERICAN SERIES

OCTAVIO PAZ

The Siren & the Seashell

AND OTHER ESSAYS ON POETS AND POETRY

TRANSLATED BY LYSANDER KEMP

AND MARGARET SAYERS PEDEN

ILLUSTRATED BY BARRY MOSER

UNIVERSITY OF TEXAS PRESS

AUSTIN

The Texas Pan American Series is published with the
assistance of a revolving publication fund established by the
Pan American Sulphur Company. Publication of this book
was also assisted by a grant from the Rockefeller Foundation
through the Latin American translation program of the
Association of American University Presses.

Library of Congress Cataloging in Publication Data

Paz, Octavio, 1914–
    "The siren and the seashell" and other essays on poets
and poetry.

    (The Texas pan American series)
    Includes bibliographical references and index.
    1. Poetry—History and criticism—Collected works.
I. Title.
PN1136.P3   809.1   75-40298
ISBN 0-292-77652-7 pbk.

Printed in the United States of America

First Paperback Edition, 1991

♾ The paper used in this publication meets the minimum
requirements of American National Standard for Information Sciences—Permanence of Paper for Printed Library
Materials, ANSI Z39.48-1984.

Contents

EDITOR'S NOTE vii

I.   Sor Juana Inés de la Cruz,
      Rubén Darío, José Juan Tablada,
      Ramón López Velarde, Alfonso Reyes

      SOR JUANA INÉS DE LA CRUZ 3
      THE SIREN AND THE SEASHELL 17
      JOSÉ JUAN TABLADA 57
      THE ROAD OF PASSION 67
      THE RIDER OF THE AIR 113

II.   Robert Frost, E. E. Cummings,
      Saint-John Perse, Antonio Machado, Jorge Guillén

      VISIT TO A POET 125
      E. E. CUMMINGS 131
      A MODERN HYMN 137
      ANTONIO MACHADO 145
      JORGE GUILLÉN 153

III.   Poetry of Solitude and Poetry of
      Communion and A Literature of Foundations

      POETRY OF SOLITUDE AND POETRY OF
      COMMUNION 163
      A LITERATURE OF FOUNDATIONS 173

      INDEX 181

Illustrations

SOR JUANA INÉS DE LA CRUZ   2

RUBÉN DARÍO   16

JOSÉ JUAN TABLADA   58

RAMÓN LÓPEZ VELARDE   66

ALFONSO REYES   114

ROBERT FROST   124

E. E. CUMMINGS   132

SAINT-JOHN PERSE   138

ANTONIO MACHADO   144

JORGE GUILLÉN   152

Editor's Note

Between 1957 and 1965 Octavio Paz published three collections of essays, articles, and reviews, mainly on poets and poetry, that had appeared in journals and elsewhere. Shortly before and after those dates he published two editions of a book of sustained reflections on the poetic phenomenon, *El arco y la lira* (Mexico City: Fondo de Cultura Económica, 1956; revised and enlarged edition, 1967). The second edition of that book has been published in English, in the translation of Ruth L. C. Simms, as *The Bow and the Lyre* (Austin: University of Texas Press, 1973). *The Siren and the Seashell*, which is made up of selections from those three collections, is intended as a companion volume to *The Bow and the Lyre*. It contains ten essays in which Paz turned his attention to individual poets, followed by two others of a more general nature.

In the first section, the poets under discussion are Latin American, all but Rubén Darío Mexican; the essays are arranged chronologically according to the birth dates of the poets. In the second section, the poets are from other parts: two from the United States, one from France, and two from Spain. In the third section, the two essays are in order of composition. One of these, "Poetry of Solitude and Poetry of Communion," written in 1942, was the seed that grew to be *The Bow and the Lyre*, which, Paz has said, in his foreword to the first edition, "is merely the maturing, the development, and, here and there, the correction of that distant text." For the reader who wishes to read all the essays in the order in which they were written, the place of composition and date are given in brackets under each title.

The essays on Darío and López Velarde are from *Cuadrivio* [Quadrivium] (Mexico City: Editorial Joaquín Mortiz, 1965); those on Sor Juana, Tablada, Frost, and Machado, and "Poetry of Solitude and Poetry of Communion," are from *Las peras del olmo* [Pears from the elm tree] (Mexico City: Universidad Nacional Autónoma de México, 1957); the rest are from *Puertas al campo* [Doors to outside] (Mexico

City: Universidad Nacional Autónoma de México, 1966). "A Literature of Foundations" was published in translation in *TriQuarterly* 13–14 (Fall–Winter 1968–1969). A much abbreviated version of the essay on Darío was published as a prologue in *Selected Poems of Rubén Darío* (Austin: University of Texas Press, 1965).

The selection and arrangement of the essays in this volume were made with the assistance and approval of the author.

L.K.

I.

Sor Juana Inés de la Cruz

Rubén Darío

José Juan Tablada

Ramón López Velarde

Alfonso Reyes

Sor Juana Inés de la Cruz

[PARIS, 1950]

In 1690, Manuel Fernández de Santa Cruz, bishop of Puebla, published Sor Juana Inés's criticism of the Jesuit Antonio de Vieyra's famous sermon, "Christ's Proofs of Love for Man." This *Carta atenagórica* [Letter worthy of Athena] is Sor Juana's only theological composition, or at least the only one that has survived.

Taken up at a friend's behest and written "with more repugnance than any other feeling, as much because it treats sacred things, for which I have reverent terror, as because it seems to wish to impugn, for which I have a natural aversion," the *Carta* had immediate repercussions. It was most unusual that a Mexican nun should dare to criticize, with as much rigor as intellectual boldness, the celebrated confessor of Christina of Sweden. But, if her criticism of Vieyra produced astonishment, her singular opinion on divine favors must have perturbed even those who admired her. Sor Juana maintained that the greatest beneficences of God are negative: "To reward is beneficence, to punish is beneficence, and to suspend beneficence is the greatest beneficence and not to perform good acts the greatest goodness." In a nun who loved poetry and science and was more preoccupied with learning than with her own salvation, this idea ran the risk of being judged as something more than theological subtlety: if the greatest divine favor were indifference, did this not too greatly enlarge the sphere of free will?

The bishop of Puebla, the nun's publisher and friend, did not conceal his disagreement. Under the pseudonym of Sor Filotea de la Cruz, he declared, in the missive that preceded the *Carta atenagórica*: "Although your discretion calls them blessings [the negative beneficences], I hold them to be punishments." Indeed, for the Christian there is no life outside of grace, and even liberty is a reflection of that grace. Moreover, the prelate did not content himself with demonstrating his lack of conformity with Sor Juana's theology but manifested a still more decided and cutting reprobation of her intellectual and literary affinities: "I do not intend that you change your nature by renouncing books, but that you better it by reading that of Jesus Christ . . . it is a pity that so great an understanding lower itself in such a way by unworthy notice of the Earth that it have not desire to penetrate what transpires in Heaven; and, since it be already lowered to the ground, that it not descend further, to consider what transpires in Hell." The bishop's letter brought Sor Juana face to face with the problem of her vocation and, more fundamentally, with her entire life. The theological discussion passed to a second plane.

Respuesta a Sor Filotea de la Cruz [Reply to Sister Filotea de la Cruz] was the last thing Sor Juana wrote. A critical autobiography, a defense of her right to learn, and a confession of the limits of all human learning, this text announced her final submission. Two years later she sold her books and abandoned herself to the powers of silence. Ripe for death, she did not escape the epidemic of 1695.[1]

I fear that it may not be possible to understand what her work and her life tell us unless first we understand the meaning of this renunciation of the word. To hear what the cessation of her voice says to us is more than a baroque formula for comprehension. For, if silence is "a negative thing," not speaking is not: the characteristic function of silence is not at all the same thing as having nothing to say. Silence is inexpressible, the sonorous expression of nothingness; not speaking is significant: even in regard to "those things one cannot say, it is needful to say at least that they cannot be said, so that it may be understood that not speaking is not ignorance of what to say, but rather is being unable to express the many things that are to be said." What is it that the last years of Sor Juana keep silent from us? And does what they keep silent belong to the realm of silence, that is, of the inexpressible, or to that of not speaking, which speaks through allusions and signs?

Sor Juana's crisis coincided with the upheaval and the public calamities that darkened the end of the seventeenth century in Mexico. It does

---

1. Among the few things found in her cell was an unfinished poem "in recognition of the inimitable writers of Europe who made their works greater by their praise."

not seem reasonable to believe that the first was an effect of the second. This kind of linear explanation necessitates another. The chain of cause and effect is endless. Furthermore, one cannot use history to explain culture as if it were a matter of different orders: one the world of facts, the other that of works. Facts are inseparable from works. Man moves in a world of works. Culture is history. And one may add that what is peculiar to history is culture and that there is no history except that of culture: the history of men's works and the history of men in their works. Thus, Sor Juana's silence and the tumultuous events of 1692 are closely related facts and are unintelligible except within the history of colonial culture. Both are consequences of a historical crisis little studied until now.

In the temporal sphere New Spain had been founded as the harmonious and hierarchical coexistence of many races and nations under the shadow of the Austrian monarchy; in the spiritual sphere, upon the universality of the Christian revelation. The superiority of the Spanish monarchy to the Aztec state was somewhat similar to that of the new religion: both constituted an open order capable of including all men and all races. The temporal order was just, moreover, because it was based upon the Christian revelation, upon the divine and rational word. Renouncing the rational word—keeping silent—and burning the Court of Justice, a symbol of the state, were acts of similar significance. In these acts New Spain expressed itself as negation. But this negation was not made against an external power: through these acts the colony negated itself and renounced its own existence, but no affirmation was born out of this negation. The poet fell silent, the intellectual abdicated, the people rebelled. The crisis led to silence. All doors were closed and colonial history was revealed as an adventure without an exit.

The meaning of the colonial crisis may be misunderstood if one yields to the temptation of considering it as a prophecy of independence. This would be true if independence were solely the extreme consequence of the dissolution of the Spanish Empire. But it was something more and also something substantially different: it was a revolution, that is, the exchange of the colonial order for another. Or say it was a complete beginning again of America's history. In spite of what many think, the colonial world did not give birth to an independent Mexico: there was a rupture and, following that, an order founded on principles and institutions radically different from the old ones.[2] That is why the nineteenth century has seemed remote from its colonial past. No one recognized himself as being in the tradition of New Spain because, in fact, the liberals who brought about independence were of a different tradition. For more than a century, Mexico has lived without a past.

If the crisis that closed the period of the Austrian monarchy did not prophesy independence, then what was its meaning? Compared to the plurality of nations and tongues that comprised the pre-Hispanic world, New Spain presented a unitarian structure: all peoples and all men had a place in that universal order. In Sor Juana's *villancicos* ("Christmas carols") a heterogeneous multitude confesses a single faith and a single loyalty, in Nahuatl, Latin, and Spanish. Colonial Catholicism was as universal as the monarchy, and all the old gods and ancient mythologies, scarcely disguised, could be accommodated in its heavens. Abandoned by their divinities, the Indians, through baptism, renewed their ties with the divine and once again found their place in this world and in the other. The uprooting effect of the Conquest was resolved into the discovery of an ultraterrestrial home. But Catholicism arrived in Mexico as a religion already formed and on the defensive. Few have pointed out that the apogee of the Catholic religion in America coincided with its European twilight: sunset there was dawn among us. The new religion was a centuries-old religion with a subtle and complex philosophy that left no door open to the ardors of investigation or the doubts of speculation. This difference in historical rhythm—the root of the crisis —is also perceivable in other orbits, from the economic to the literary. In all orders the situation was similar: there was nothing to invent, nothing to add, nothing to propose. Scarcely born, New Spain was an opulent flower condemned to a premature and static maturity. Sor Juana embodies this maturity. Her poetry is an excellent showcase of sixteenth- and seventeenth-century styles. Assuredly, at times—as in her imitation of Jacinto Polo de Medina—she is superior to her model, but

2. It is true that many colonial traits were prolonged until 1857—even to our own time—but as inertia, obstacles, and obstinate survival, like facts that have lost their historical meaning.

she discovered no new worlds. The same is true of her theater, and the greatest praise one can offer of *El divino Narciso* [The divine Narcissus] is that it is not unworthy of the Calderonian sacramental plays. (Only in *Primero sueño* [First dream], for reasons that will be examined later, does she surpass her masters.) In short, Sor Juana never transcended the style of her epoch. It was not possible for her to break those forms that imprisoned her so subtly and within which she moved with such elegance: to destroy them would have been to repudiate her own being. The conflict was insoluble because her only escape would have demanded the destruction of the very foundations of the colonial world.

As it was not possible to deny the principles on which that society rested without repudiating oneself, it was also impossible to propose others. Neither the tradition nor the history of New Spain could propose alternative solutions. It is true that two centuries later other principles were adopted, but one must remember that they came from outside, from France and the United States, and would form a different society. At the end of the seventeenth century the colonial world lost any possibility of renewing itself: the same principles that had engendered it were now choking it.

Denying this world and affirming another were acts that could not have the same significance for Sor Juana that they had for the great spirits of the Counter Reformation or the evangelists of New Spain. For Saints Theresa and Ignatius, renunciation of this world did not signify resignation or silence, but a change of destiny: history, and human action with it, opened to the other world and thus acquired new fecundity. The mystic life did not consist so much of quitting this world as of introducing personal life into sacred history. Militant Catholicism, evangelical or reformist, impregnated history with meaning, and the negation of the world was translated finally into an affirmation of historical action. In contrast, the truly personal portion of Sor Juana's work does not touch upon either action or contemplation, but upon knowledge—a knowledge that questions this world but does not judge it. This new kind of knowledge was impossible within the tenets of her historical universe. For more than twenty years Sor Juana adhered to her purpose. And she did not yield until all doors were definitely closed. Within herself the conflict was radical: knowledge is dream. When history awakened her from her dream, at the end of her life, she ceased to speak. Her awakening closed the golden dream of the viceroyship. If we do not understand her silence, we cannot comprehend what *Primero sueño* and *Respuesta a Sor Filotea de la Cruz* really mean: knowledge is impossible, and all utterance flows into silence. In understanding her silence one

> *deciphers glories*
> *amid characters of devastation.*

Ambiguous glories. Everything in her—vocation, soul, body—was ambivalent. While she was still a child her family sent her to live in Mexico City with relatives. At sixteen she was lady-in-waiting to the Marquesa de Mancera, vicereine of New Spain. Through the biography by Father P. Diego Calleja we are able to hear the echoes of the celebrations and competitions in which the young prodigy Juana shone. Beautiful and alone, she was not without suitors. But she chose not to be the "white wall upon which all would throw mud." She took the habit, because, "considering my totally negative attitude toward matrimony, it seemed the most fitting and most decent thing I could choose." We know now that she was an illegitimate child. Had she been legitimate, would she have chosen married life? This possibility is dubious. When Sor Juana speaks of her intellectual vocation she seems sincere: neither the absence of worldly love nor the urgency of divine love led her to the cloister. The convent was an expedient, a reasonable solution, offering refuge and solitude. The cell was an asylum, not a hermit's cave. Laboratory, library, salon, there she received visitors and conversed with them; poems were read, discussions held, and good music heard. She participated from the convent in both intellectual and courtly life. She was constantly writing poetry. She wrote plays, Christmas carols, prologues, treatises on music, and reflections on morality. Between the viceregal palace and the convent flowed a constant exchange of rhymes and civilities, compliments, satirical poems, and petitions. Indulged child, the tenth Muse.

"The tender phrases of the Mexican language" appear in her *villancicos* along with black Congolese and the unpolished speech of the

Basque. With complete awareness, and even a certain coquetry, Sor Juana employs all those rare spices:

> *What magic infusions*
> *known to the Indian herbsmen*
> *of my country spread their enchantment*
> *among my writings?*

We would be in error if we confused the baroque aesthetic—which opened doors to the exoticism of the New World—with a preoccupation with nationalism. Actually one might say precisely the opposite. This predilection for languages and native dialects—in imitation of Luis de Góngora—does not so much reveal a hypothetical divination of future nationalism as a lively consciousness of the universality of the empire: Indians, Creoles, mulattoes, and Spaniards form one whole. Her preoccupation with pre-Columbian religions—apparent in the prologue to *El divino Narciso*—has similar meaning. The functions of the church were no different from those of the empire: to conciliate antagonisms and to embrace all differences in one superior truth.

Love is one of the constant themes in her poetry. Scholars say that she loved and was loved. She herself tells us this in various lyrics and sonnets—although in *Respuesta a Sor Filotea de la Cruz* she warns us that everything she wrote, except for *Primero sueño*, was commissioned. It is of little importance whether these were her loves or another's, whether they were experienced or imagined: by the grace of her poetry she made them her own. Her eroticism is intellectual; by that I do not mean that it is lacking in either profundity or authenticity. Like all great lovers, Sor Juana delights in the dialectic of passion; also, for she is sensual, in its rhetoric, which is not the same as the rhetorical passions of some female poets. The men and women in her poems are images, shadows "fashioned by fantasy." Her Platonism is not exempt from ardor. She feels her body is like a sexless flame:

> *And I know that my body—*
> *never inclining to one or the other—*
> *is neuter, or abstract, everything*
> *the soul alone safekeeps.*

The question is a burning one. Thus she leaves it "so that others may air it," since one should not attempt subtleties about things that are best ignored. No less ambiguous is her attitude toward the two sexes. The men of her sonnets and lyrics are fleeting shadows exemplifying absence and disdain. However, her portraits of women are splendid, especially those of the vicereines who protected her, the Marquesa de Mancera and the Condesa de Paredes. Sor Juana's poem that "paints the beautiful proportions of the Lady Paredes" is one of the memorable works of Gongoristic poetry. This passion should not scandalize:

> *To be a woman and to be absent*
> *is no impediment to loving you,*
> *for souls, as you know,*
> *ignore distance and gender.*

The same rationale appears in almost all her amorous poetry—and also in the poems that treat the friendship she professes for Phyllis or Lysis: "Pure love, without desire for indecencies, can feel what profanest love feels." It would be excessive to speak of homosexuality; it is not excessive to observe that she herself does not hide the ambiguity of her feelings. In one of her most profound sonnets she repeats:

> *Though you may thwart the tight bond*
> *that enclasped your fantastic form,*
> *it is little use to evade arms and breast*
> *if my fantasy builds you a prison.*

Her loves, real or imagined, were without doubt chaste. She loved the body with her soul, but who can trace the boundaries between one and the other? For us, body and soul are one, or almost so: our idea of the body is colored by the spirit, and vice versa. Sor Juana lived in a world based on dualism, and for her the problem was easier to resolve, as much in the sphere of ideas as in that of conduct. When the Marquesa de Mancera died, she asked:

> *Beauteous compound, in Laura divided,*
> *immortal soul, glorious spirit,*

why leave a body so beautiful,
and why bid farewell to such a soul?

Sor Juana moved among shadows: those of untouchable bodies and fleeting souls. For her, only divine love was both concrete and ideal. But Sor Juana is not a mystic poet, and in her religious poems divinity is an abstraction. God is Idea and Concept, and even where she visibly follows the mystics she resists mixing the earthly and the heavenly. Divine love is rational love.

These were not her great love. From the time of her childhood she was inclined toward learning. As an adolescent she conceived the project of dressing as a man and attending the university. Resigned to being self-taught, she complained: "How hard it is to study those soulless marks on the page, lacking the living voice of the master." And she added that all these labors "were suffered for the love of learning; oh, had it only been for the love of God—which were proper—how worthwhile it would have been!" This lament is a confession: the knowledge she seeks is not in sacred books. If theology is the "queen of the sciences," she lingers on her outer skirts: physics and logic, rhetoric and law. But her curiosity is not that of the specialist; she aspires to the integration of individual truths and insists upon the unity of learning. Variety does not harm general understanding; rather, it exacts it; all sciences are related: "It is the chain the ancients imagined issuing from the mouth of Jupiter, from which all things were suspended, linked one with another."

Her interest in science is impressive. In the lines of *Primero sueño* she describes, with a pedantry that makes us smile, the alimentary functions, the phenomenon of sleep and fantasy, the curative value of certain poisons, the Egyptian pyramids, and the magic lantern that

reproduces, feigned
on the white wall, various figures,
helped no less by the shadows
than by light in tremulous reflections . . .

Everything blends together: theology, science, baroque rhetoric, and true astonishment before the universe. Her attitude is rare in the Hispanic tradition. For the great Spaniards learning resolved into either heroic action or negation of the world (positive negation, to state it differently). For Sor Juana the world is a problem. For her, everything stimulates questions; her whole being is one excited question. The universe is a vast labyrinth within which the soul can find no unraveling thread, "shifting sands making it impossible for those attempting to follow a course." Nothing is further removed from this rational puzzle than the image of the world left us by the Spanish classics. There, science and action are blended. To learn is to act, and all action, like all learning, is related to the world beyond. Within this tradition disinterested learning is blasphemy or madness.

The church did not judge Sor Juana mad or blasphemous, but it did lament her deviation. In *Respuesta a Sor Filotea de la Cruz* she tells us that "they mortified and tormented me by saying, These studies are not in conformance with saintly ignorance, she will be lost, she will faint away at such heights in her own perspicacity and acuity." Double solitude: that of the conscience and that of being a woman. A superior— "very saintly and very candid, who believed that study was a matter for the Inquisition"—ordered her not to study. Her confessor tightened the ring and for two years denied her spiritual assistance. It was difficult to resist so much opposing pressure, as before it had been difficult not to be disoriented by the adulation of the court. Sor Juana persisted. Using the texts of the church fathers as support, she defended her right—and that of all women—to knowledge. And not only to learning, but also to teaching: "What is unseemly in an elderly woman's having as her charge the education of young ladies?"

Versatile, attracted by a thousand things at once, she defended herself by studying, and, studying, she retreated. If her superiors took away her books, she still had her mind, that consumed more matter in a quarter of an hour than books in four years. Not even in sleep was she liberated "from this continuous movement of my imagination; rather it is wont to work more freely, less encumbered, in my sleep . . . arguing and making verses that would fill a very large catalogue." This is one of her most beautiful confessions and one that gives us the key to her major poem: dreaming is a longer and more lucid wakefulness. Dreaming is knowing. In addition to diurnal learning arises another, necessarily rebellious form of learning, beyond the law and subject to a punishment that stimulates the spirit more than it terrorizes it. I need not emphasize here how the concept that governs *Primero sueño* coincides with some of modern poetry's preoccupations.

We owe the best and clearest description of the subject matter of *Primero sueño* to Father Calleja's biography: "It being nighttime, I slept. I dreamed that once and for all I desired to understand all the things that comprise the universe: I could not, not even as they are divided into categories, not even an individual one. The dawn came and, disillusioned, I awoke." Sor Juana declared that she wrote the poem as a deliberate imitation of *Soledades* [Solitudes]. But *Primero sueño* is a poem about nocturnal astonishment, while Góngora's poem is about daytime. There is nothing behind the images of the Cordovan poet because his world is pure image, a splendor of appearances. Sor Juana's universe—barren of color, abounding in shadows, abysses, and sudden clearings—is a labyrinth of symbols, a rational delirium. *Primero sueño* is a poem about knowledge. This distinguishes it from Gongoristic poetry and, more finally, from all baroque poetry. This very quality binds it, unexpectedly, to German Romantic poetry and through that to the poetry of our own time.

In some passages the baroque verse resists the unusual exercise of transcribing concepts and abstract formulas into images. The language becomes abrupt and pedantic. In other lines, the best and most intense, expression becomes dizzying in its lucidity. Sor Juana creates an abstract and hallucinatory landscape formed of cones, obelisks, pyramids, geometric precipices, and aggressive peaks. Her world partakes of mechanics and of myth. The sphere and the triangle rule its empty sky. Poetry of science, but also of nocturnal terror. The poem begins when night reigns over the world. Everything sleeps, overcome by dreams. The king and the thief sleep, the lovers and the solitary. The body lies delivered unto itself. Diminished life of the body, disproportionate life of the spirit, freed from its corporeal weight. Nourishment, transformed into heat, engenders sensations that fantasy converts into images. On the heights of her mental pyramid—formed by all the powers of the spirit, memory and imagination, judgment and fantasy—the soul contemplates the phantasms of the world and, especially, those figures of the mind, "the clear intellectual stars" of her interior sky. In them the soul re-creates itself in itself. Later, the soul dissociates itself from this contemplation and spreads its gaze over all creation; the world's diversity dazzles it and finally blinds it. An intellectual eagle, the soul hurls itself from the precipice "into the neutrality of a sea of astonishment." The fall does not annihilate it. Incapable of flight, it climbs. Painfully, step by step, it ascends the pyramid. Since method must repair the "defect of being unable to know all of creation in an intuitive act," it divides the world into categories, grades of knowledge. *Primero sueño* describes the progress of thought, a spiral that ascends from the inanimate toward man and his symbol, the triangle, a figure in which animal and divine converge. Man is the site of creation's rendezvous, life's highest point of tension, always between two abysses: "lofty lowliness . . . at the mercy of amorous union." But method does not remedy the limitations of the spirit. Understanding cannot discern the ties that unite the inanimate to the animate, vegetable to animal, animal to man. Nor is it even feasible to penetrate the most simple phenomenon: the individual is as irreducible as the species. Darkly it realizes that the immense variety of creation is resolved in one law but that that law is ineffable. The soul vacillates. Perhaps it would be better to retreat. Examples of other defeats rise up as a warning to the imprudent. The warning becomes a challenge; the spirit becomes inflamed as it sees that others did not hesitate to "make their names eternal in their ruin." The poem is peopled with Promethean images; the act of knowing, not knowledge itself, is the battle prize. The fallen soul affirms itself and, making cajolery of its terror, hastens to elect new courses. In that instant the fasting body reclaims its own dominion. The sun bursts forth. Images dissolve. Knowledge is a dream. But the sun's victory is partial and cyclical. It triumphs in half the world; in the other half it is vanquished. Rebellious night, "recovered by reason of its fall," erects its empire in the territories the sun forsakes. There, other souls dream Sor Juana's dream. The universe the poem reveals to us is ambivalent: wakefulness is dream; the night's defeat, its victory. The dream of knowledge also means: knowledge is dream. Each affirmation carries within it its own negation.

Sor Juana's night is not the carnal night of lovers. Neither is it the night of the mystics. It is an intellectual night, lofty and fixed like an immense eye, a night firmly constructed above the void, rigorous geometry, taciturn obelisk, all of it fixed tension directed toward the heavens. This vertical impulse is the only thing that recalls other nights of Spanish mysticism. But the mystics seem to be attracted to heaven by lines of celestial forces, as one sees in certain of El Greco's paintings. In *Primero sueño* the heavens are closed; the heights are hostile to flight. Silence confronting man: the desire for knowledge is illicit and the soul that dreams of knowledge is rebellious. Nocturnal solitude of the consciousness. Drought, vertigo, palpitation. But, nevertheless, all is not adversity. In his solitude and his fall from the heights man affirms himself in himself: to know is to dream, but that dream is everything we know of ourselves, and in that dream resides our greatness. It is a game of mirrors in which the soul loses each time it wins and wins each time it loses, and the poem's emotion springs from the awareness of this ambiguity. Sor Juana's cyclical and vertiginous night suddenly reveals its fixed center: *Primero sueño* is a poem not of knowledge but of the *act of knowing*. And thus Sor Juana transmutes her historical and personal ill fortunes, makes victory of her defeat, song of her silence. Once again poetry is nourished by history and biography. Once again it transcends them.

M.S.P.

The Siren and the Seashell

[DELHI, 1964]

. . . the race
that creates life with the Pythagorean numbers.
                                    Rubén Darío

According to the textbooks, the sixteenth and seventeenth centuries were the golden age of Spanish literature. Juan Ramón Jiménez has said that they were not gold but gilded cardboard. It would be fairer to say that they were the centuries of Spanish rage. The Spaniards wrote, painted, and dreamed in the same frenzy in which they destroyed and created nations. Everything was carried to extremes: they were the first to circumnavigate the earth, and at the same time they were the inventors of quietism. A thirst for space, a hunger for death. Lope de Vega was prolific, even profligate: he wrote something over one thousand plays. Saint John of the Cross was temperate, even miserly: his poetical works consist of three longish lyrics and a few songs and ballads. A delirium, whether boisterous or reserved, bloodthirsty or pious: in all colors, in all directions. The lucid delirium of Cervantes, Velázquez, Calderón. Quevedo's labyrinth of conceits. Góngora's jungle of verbal stalactites. And then, suddenly, the stage was bare, as if the whole performance had been a magician's show rather than historical reality. Nothing was left, nothing but ghostly reflections. During all of the eighteenth century there was no Swift or Pope, no Rousseau or Laclos, anywhere in Spanish literature. In the second half of the nineteenth century a few faint signs of life began to appear: Gustavo Bécquer, Rosalía de Castro. But there was no one to compare with Coleridge, Leopardi, Hölderlin, no one resembled Baudelaire. Then, at the close of the century, everything changed again, just as violently. A new group of poets burst onto the scene without warning; at the beginning, few listened to them and many jeered. But a few years later, through the efforts of the very figures whom the "serious" critics had called Frenchified outsiders, the Spanish language was on its feet, alive again. Not so opulent as it had been during the baroque period, but stronger, clearer, better controlled.

The last major baroque poet was a Mexican nun, Sor Juana Inés de la Cruz. Two centuries later, the revival of Spanish literature, and of the language itself, was also begun here in the New World. The movement known as Modernism had a double importance: on the one hand, it produced four or five poets who linked up the great chain of Spanish tradition that had come apart at the end of the seventeenth century; on the other hand, it opened windows and doors so that the fresh air of the times could revive the language. Modernism was not merely a school of poetry; it was also a dancing class, a gymnasium, a circus, and a masked ball. After that experience, the language could put up with the most strenuous tests, the most dangerous escapades. If we recognize Modernism for what it really was—a movement whose foundations and primordial goal were the movement itself—we can see that it has not yet ended: the vanguard of 1925 and the efforts of contemporary poets are intimately linked to that great beginning. In its day, Modernism aroused fervid support and no less vehement opposition. A few writers received it with reserve: Miguel de Unamuno did not disguise his hostility, and Antonio Machado kept his distance. No matter: both of them were affected by Modernism. Their poetry would be different without the discoveries and conquests of the Spanish American poets; and their diction, above all when they tried most ostensibly to avoid the accents and modes of the innovators, is a sort of involuntary homage to the very movement it rejects. Their work is inseparable from what it denies, precisely because it is a reaction: it is not *beyond* Rubén Darío but is *facing* him. That is natural enough: Modernism was the language of the epoch, its historical style, and all creators were condemned to breathe its atmosphere.

Every language, not excluding that of liberty, eventually becomes a prison, and there is a point in the process at which speed becomes confused with immobility. The great Modernist poets were the first to rebel, and in their mature work they go beyond the language that they themselves had created. Therefore, each in his own way prepared for the subversion of the vanguard: Leopoldo Lugones was the immediate antecedent of the new poetry in Mexico (Ramón López Velarde) and Argentina (Jorge Luis Borges); Juan Ramón Jiménez was the guiding spirit of the generation of Jorge Guillén and Federico García Lorca; Ramón del Valle-Inclán is a presence in the modern theater and will daily become more influential. Darío's place is central, even if one believes, as I do, that of the great Modernists he is least a presence. He is not a living force but a point of reference, a point of departure or arrival, a boundary that has to be reached or crossed. To be like him or not: either way, Darío is present in the spirit of contemporary poets. He is the founder.

The history of Modernism extends from 1880 to 1910 and has been recounted many times. I will mention only what is essential. With two or three minor exceptions, Spanish and Spanish American Romanticism gave us few works of any note. None of our Romantic poets had a clear awareness of what that great change really signified. In Spanish, Romanticism was a school of rebellion and oratory, but it was not a vision in the meaning that Arnim gave to the word: "We call sacred poets seers, we call poetic creation a superior kind of vision." With these words, Romanticism proclaimed the superiority of poetic vision to religious revelation. We were also lacking in irony, which is something very different from sarcasm or invective: separation of the object by the insertion of the I; disillusionment with the consciousness, which is unable to annul the distance that separates it from the world outside; an insensate dialogue between the infinite I and finite space or between mortal man and the immortal universe. Furthermore, there was no recognition of the alliance between dreaming and waking, no presentiment that reality is a constellation of symbols, no belief in the creative imagination as the prime faculty of understanding. In sum, a lack of awareness of the divided self and its desire for unity. The poverty of our Romanticism becomes even more disconcerting when we recall that for the German and English poets Spain was the chosen land of the Romantic spirit. The Jena group discovered Calderón; Shelley translated fragments of his theater; and one of the central books of German Romanticism, the powerful and fascinating *Titan*, is impregnated with irony, magic, and other fantastic elements that Jean Paul probably drew from one of the least studied (and most modern) works of Cervantes, *Los trabajos de Persiles y Segismunda* [The misfortunes of Persiles and Segismunda]. When Romanticism flickered out, there was nothing left, and Spanish literature oscillated between oratory and chit-chat, academia and the café.

The inspiration for our Romantic writers had come from France. Although it is true that French Romanticism did not produce writers comparable to those of Germany and England (if we except Gérard de Nerval, and the Victor Hugo of *La fin de Satan*), the succeeding generation produced a group of works in which the aims of Romanticism were both achieved and transcended. Baudelaire and his great descendants gave Romanticism a new consciousness, a *significant form*. Also, and above all, they made poetry a total experience, at once verbal and spiritual. For them the word did not merely speak the world; it also established it—or changed it. The poem became a space inhabited by living symbols; the written language was brought to life by the anima, the soul.

During the last third of the nineteenth century, the frontiers of poetry—the frontiers of the unknown—were in France. In the works of French poets the Romantic inspiration turned in on itself, contemplated itself. Enthusiasm, which for Novalis was the origin of poetry, changed into the reflectiveness of Mallarmé; the divided consciousness took revenge on the object for being opaque by eliminating it. But Spanish writers, despite their nearness to that magnetic center that was French poetry (or, perhaps, because of their nearness), were not attracted by the adventures of those years. On the other hand, the Spanish Americans, dissatisfied with the pretentious prattle emanating from Spain, understood that nothing personal could be said in a language that had lost the secret of metamorphosis and surprise. They felt themselves to be different from the Spaniards and turned almost instinctively toward France, divining that not a new world but a new language was being born there. They made that language their own in order to be more themselves, in order to say what they wanted to say. Hence the main accomplishment of the reforms carried out by the Spanish American Modernists was to appropriate and assimilate modern European poetry. Their immediate model was French poetry, not only because it was the most accessible but also because they saw in it, rightly, the most compelling, audacious, and complete expression of the tendencies of the period.

In its first phase, Modernism was not an organized movement. Isolated figures appeared in various places, almost at the same time: José Martí in New York, Julián del Casal in Havana, Manuel Gutiérrez Nájera and Salvador Díaz Mirón in Mexico City, José Asunción Silva in Bogotá, Rubén Darío in Santiago de Chile. They soon came to know one another and to realize that their individual efforts were part of a general change in sensibility and language. Little by little they formed small groups and even published their own magazines, such as Gutiérrez Nájera's *Revista Azul* [Blue review]; the diffuse tendencies crystallized and two centers of activity were formed, one in Buenos Aires, the other in Mexico City. This period has been called the second generation of Modernism. Rubén Darío was the point of connection between the two periods. The premature deaths of most of the initiators, and his gifts as critic and stimulus, made him the recognized leader of the movement. More clearly than had their precursors the new poets understood that their work was the first truly independent expression in Spanish American literature. They were not intimidated when traditional critics called them outsiders: they knew that no one finds himself until he has left his birthplace.

The French influence was predominant but not exclusive. With the exception of Martí, who knew and loved the literature of England and the United States, and Silva, "impassioned reader of Nietzsche, Baudelaire, and Mallarmé,"[1] the first Modernists went on from the cult of French Romanticism to that of Parnassianism. The second generation, in full development, "added to the Parnassian style, which was rich in vision, the Symbolist style, which was rich in music."[2] Their curiosity was both extensive and intense, but at times their enthusiasm clouded their judgment. They were equally impressed by Gautier and Mendès, Heredia and Mallarmé. A good indication of their preferences can be

1. Max Henríquez Ureña, *Breve historia del modernismo* (Mexico City, 1962).

2. Enrique Anderson Imbert, *Historia de la literatura hispanoamericana* (Mexico City, 1962).

found in the series of literary portraits that Rubén Darío published in an Argentine newspaper, almost all of them later brought together in *Los raros* [The rare ones] (1896). In these articles the names of Poe, Villiers de l'Isle-Adam, Bloy, Nietzsche, Verlaine, Rimbaud, and Lautréamont are jumbled together with those of minor or now-forgotten writers. Only one of the figures he discusses wrote in the Spanish language, the Cuban José Martí. There is also a Portuguese, Eugenio de Castro, the initiator of free verse in Portugal. In some cases Darío's instincts were amazing: he was the first person outside of France to be interested in Lautréamont. (In France itself, if I remember correctly, only Léon Bloy and Remy de Gourmont had written earlier about Lautréamont. Also, I suspect that Darío was the first person writing in Spanish to allude to Sade, in a sonnet dedicated to Valle-Inclán.) Many other names must of course be added to this list. It will suffice to mention the most important. First of all, Baudelaire, and then Jules Laforgue, both of them decisive in the development of the second generation of Modernists; the Belgian Symbolists; Stefan George, Wilde, and Swinburne; and, more as an example and stimulus than as a direct model, Whitman. Although not all his idols were French, Darío once said—perhaps to annoy the Spanish critics who accused him of mental Gallicism—that "Modernism is nothing else but Castilian prose and verse passed through the fine sieve of good French prose and verse." But it would be a mistake to reduce the movement to a mere imitation of France. The originality of Modernism does not lie in its mastery of influences but in its own creations.

Beginning in 1888, Darío used the word "Modernism" to designate the tendencies of the Spanish American poets. In 1898 he wrote: "The new spirit that today animates a small but proud and triumphant group of Spanish American writers and poets: Modernism." Later he would say "the moderns," "modernity." During his long and extensive activities as a critic he never stopped repeating that the distinctive characteristic of the new poets, their reason for being, was the will to be modern. Somewhat as the term "vanguard" is a metaphor revealing a conception of literary activities as warfare, the term "Modernist" reveals a kind of ingenuous faith in the superiority of the future or, to be more exact, of the present. The first implies a spatial vision of literature; the second, a temporal conception. The vanguard wants to conquer a location; Modernism seeks to locate itself in the present. Only those who feel that they are not wholly in the present, who sense that they are outside of living history, postulate contemporaneity as a goal. To be a contemporary of Goethe or Tamerlane is a coincidence, happy or otherwise, in which one's will plays no part; to desire to be their contemporary implies a will to participate, intellectually, in the actions of history, to share a history that belongs to others but that one somehow makes one's own. It is an affinity and a distance—and an awareness of that situation. The Modernists did not want to be French: they wanted to be modern. Technological progress had partially eliminated the distance between America and Europe. That nearness made our remoteness more vivid and perceptible. A trip to Paris or London was not a visit to another continent but a leap to another century. It has been said that Modernism was an evasion of American realities. It would be more accurate to say that it was a flight from the local present—which was, in their eyes, an anachronism—and a search for the universal present, which is the only true one. Modernity and cosmopolitanism were synonymous to Rubén Darío and his friends. They were not anti–Latin American; they wanted a Latin America that would be contemporaneous with Paris and London.

The purest, most immediate manifestation of time is the now. Time is that which is passing: the present. Geographic and historical remoteness, exoticism and archaism, fuse in an instantaneous present at the touch of actuality: they become presence. The attraction for the Modernists of the most distant past and the most remote countries—medieval and Byzantine legends and figures from pre-Columbian America and the Orient that in those years the European sensibility was discovering or inventing—was one of the forms of their appetite for the present. However, they were not fascinated by the machine, the essence of the modern world, but by the creations of Art Nouveau. Modernity for them was not industry but luxury. Instead of the straight line, Aubrey Beardsley's arabesques. Their mythology was that of Gustave Moreau (to whom Julián del Casal dedicated a group of sonnets); their secret paradises, those of the Huysmans of *A rebours* [Against the grain]; their hells, those of Poe and Baudelaire. A Marxist would say, with

some justice, that it was a literature of the leisure class, with no historical mission, soon to be extinguished. One could reply that their rejection
of the useful and their exaltation of art as the supreme good were something more than the hedonism of landholders: they were a rebellion
against social pressures and a critique of the abject realities that prevailed in Latin America. Besides, in some of these poets we find political
radicalism alongside the most extreme aesthetic positions: it is hardly
necessary to mention José Martí, the liberator of Cuba, and Manuel
González Prada of Peru, one of our first anarchists. Leopoldo Lugones
was one of the founders of Argentine socialism, and many of the Modernists participated actively in the historical struggles of their day:
Guillermo Valencia and José María Vargas Vila in Colombia, José
Santos Chocano in Peru, and Salvador Díaz Mirón in Mexico. Modernism was not a school of political abstention but of artistic purity.
Their aestheticism did not spring from moral indifference. Nor was it
hedonism. Art was for them a passion, in the religious sense of the word,
and like all passions it demanded a sacrifice. Their love for modernity
was not a cult of the fashionable, but rather a will to participate in a
historical plenitude that until then had been denied to Latin Americans.
Modernity was simply history in its richest, most immediate form. Also,
however, most painful: the moment swollen with omens, way of access
to the actions of time. It was contemporaneity. Modernist art, decadent
and barbaric, is a multitude of historical times, from the newest to the
most ancient and from the nearest to the most distant, a totality of
presences that the consciousness can take hold of at a single moment:

> *and very eighteenth century and very ancient*
> *and very modern; daring, cosmopolitan . . .*

It is still paradoxical that Spanish American poetry, almost as soon
as it was born, declared itself to be cosmopolitan. What was the name of
that cosmopolis? It was the city of cities: Nineveh, Paris, New York,
Buenos Aires. It was the most transparent and deceptive form of actuality, since it had no name and occupied no location in space. Modernism
was an abstract passion, although its poets amused themselves by accu-
mulating all sorts of rare objects. Those objects were signs, not symbols:
something interchangeable. Masks, a succession of masks that hid a

tense, avid, perpetually questioning face. The Modernists' inordinate love for full and rounded forms, for sumptuous clothing and multicolored worlds, reveals an obsession. What those brilliant, sonorous metaphors express is not love for life but *horror vacui*. That perpetual search for the strange on condition that it be new—and of the new on condition that it be unique—was a hunger for presence rather than for the present. If Modernism was an appetite for time, its best poets knew that theirs was a disembodied time. At first glance, actuality seems to be a plenitude of times, but it turns out to be lacking, deserted, inhabited by neither the past nor the future. Modernism was a movement condemned to deny itself because the movement was its only affirmation; it was an empty myth, an uninhabited soul, a nostalgia for true presence. That is the constant and central theme, the secret and never wholly enunciated theme, of the best Modernist poets.

Every revolution, including those in the arts, postulates a future that is also a return. At the Feast of the Goddess Reason the Jacobins celebrated the destruction of an unjust present and the imminent arrival of a golden age anterior to history: Rousseau's natural society. The revolutionary future is a privileged manifestation of cyclical time, announcing the return of an archetypal past. Hence, revolutionary action par excellence—the break with the immediate past and the establishment of a new order—is at the same time a restoration, that of an immemorial past, the origin of the ages. Revolution signifies return or repetition, both in the original meaning of the word—the rotation of the stars and other bodies—and in the meaning given it by our view of history. It is something more profound than a mere survival of archaic thought. Engels himself could not resist this almost spontaneous tendency in our thinking and decided that the first stage of human evolution was Morgan's "primitive communism." Revolution frees us from the old order so that the primigenial order may reappear on a higher historical level. The future that the revolutionary proposes to us is a promise: the fulfillment of something that lies hidden, a seed of life, in the origin of the ages. The revolutionary order is the end of the bad ages and the beginning of the true age. That beginning is indeed a start, but above all it is an origin. Furthermore, it is the very foundation of time. Whatever it is called—reason, justice, brotherhood, natural harmony, the logic of history—it is something that is prior to historical times or that in some manner determines them. It is the principle[3] par excellence, ruling what comes to pass. The gravitational force of time, that which gives meaning to its motion and fecundity to its turmoils, is a fixed point: that past that is a perpetual beginning.

Although the Modernists sang of the perpetual advent of the now, of its embodiment in this or that glorious or terrible form, their time marked time; it ran, but without moving. It lacked a future because it had been deprived of a past. Modernism was an aesthetic of luxury and death, a nihilistic aesthetic. However, that nihilism was more lived than assumed, more an affliction of the sensibilities than a confrontation by the spirit. A few of the Modernists, Darío first, recognized that the movement was simply a spin in the void, a mask with which the despairing consciousness both calmed and exacerbated itself. Their search, when it really was a search and not mere dissipation, was nostalgia for an origin. Man pursues his own self when he runs after this or that phantom: he seeks his beginning. Almost as soon as Modernism began to contemplate itself, it ceased to exist as a tendency. The collective adventure reached its end and individual exploration began. It was the supreme moment of the Modernist passion, the instant of lucidity that was also the instant of death.

Search for an origin, recovery of an inheritance: it might seem that nothing could be more unlike the earliest tendencies of the movement. In 1896, filled with reformist zeal, Darío cried: "The new American poets who write in Spanish have had to move swiftly from the mental independence of Spain . . . to the current that today, throughout the world, unites those distinguished groups that make up the cultivation and the life of a cosmopolitan and universal art." Unlike the Spaniards, Darío did not place the universal in opposition to the cosmopolitan; on the contrary, he held that the new art was universal because it was cosmopolitan. It was the art of the great city. Modern society, he said, "builds a Tower of Babel in which everyone understands everyone

3. The word *principio* is here italicized in the original to indicate that two of its meanings—"beginning" and "principle"—are intended.—*Trans.*

else." (I am not sure that the same is true in the new Babels, but contemporary reality, as one can see from the history of twentieth-century artistic movements, confirms Darío's view of the cosmopolitan character of modern art.) His opposition to Hispanism was a part of his love for modernity, and thus his criticism of the tradition was a criticism of Spain. His anti-Spanish attitude had a dual origin. On the one hand, it expressed a determination to break away from the ancient metropolis: "Our movement has given us a place apart, independent of Castilian literature." On the other, it identified Hispanism with traditionalism: "The evolution that brought Castilian to this renascence had to take place in America, since Spain is walled about by tradition, fenced and bristling with Hispanism."

Modernism, a verbal reform, was a syntax, a prosody, a vocabulary. Its poets enriched the language with imports from French and English; they made excessive use of archaisms and neologisms; and they were the first to employ the language of conversation. Furthermore, it is often forgotten that the Modernists' poems contain a great many Americanisms and indigenisms. Their cosmopolitanism could include both the achievements of the French naturalistic novel and American linguistic forms. A part of their lexicon has become as dated as the furniture and other objects of Art Nouveau; the rest has entered the mainstream of the language. Instead of attacking the syntax of Castilian, the Modernists restored its naturalness and avoided Latinate inversions and overemphasis. They exaggerated rather than inflated; they were often slightly ridiculous but never rigid. In spite of their swans and gondolas, they gave Spanish poetry a flexibility and familiarity that were never vulgar and that would lend themselves admirably to the two main tendencies of contemporary poetry: a love for the unexpected image and for poetic prosaicness.

Their reforms affected prosody above all, for Modernism was a prodigious exploration of the rhythmic possibilities of our language. The Modernist poets' interest in metrical problems embraced both theory and practice. Some of them wrote treatises on versification: Manuel González Prada pointed out that Castilian meters are formed of binary, ternary, and quaternary elements, rising or falling; Ricardo Jaimes

Freyre wrote that it was a matter of prosodic periods of no more than nine syllables. For both poets the beat of the tonic accent was the essential element of verse. They were both inspired by the doctrine of Andrés Bello, who as early as 1835 had said, contrary to predominant opinion, that each metric unit is composed of prosodic phrases—something similar to Greek and Roman feet but determined by accentuation rather than by syllabic quantity. Thus Modernism renewed the tradition of irregular versification that was as old as the language itself, as Pedro Henríquez Ureña has shown. But theoretical conclusions were not the origin of metric reform; rather, they were the natural consequence of poetic activity. In short, the novelty of Modernism consisted in the invention of meters; its originality, in the resurrection of accentuated rhythm.

In its use of rhythm, as in everything else, our Romanticism stopped halfway along the road. The Modernist poets assimilated the Romantic tendency toward greater rhythmic liberty and subjected it to a discipline learned in France. The French example was not the only one. The rhythmic translations of Poe, Germanic verse, the influence of Eugenio de Castro, and the reading of Whitman were all antecedents to the first semifree poems; and toward the end of Modernism the Mexican José Juan Tablada, precursor of the vanguard, introduced the haiku, a form that undoubtedly influenced Juan Ramón Jiménez and perhaps even Antonio Machado, as any attentive reader can attest. It is pointless to enumerate all the experiments and innovations of the Modernists: the resurrection of the anapestic and Provençal hendecasyllables; the breaking up of the rigid division of the hemistichs of the alexandrine line, thanks to enjambment; the vogue of nine- and twelve-syllable lines; the changes in accentuation; the invention of long lines (up to twenty or more syllables); the mixture of different measures with the same syllabic base (ternary or quaternary); ametric lines; the return to traditional forms like the Galician-Portuguese *cosante* . . . The richness of Modernist rhythms is unique in the history of the language and its reforms prepared the way for the prose poem and free verse. What I want most to emphasize is that cosmopolitanism led Latin American poets to attempt many new graftings and cross-pollinations and that those experiences revealed to them the true tradition of Spanish poetry: rhythmic versification. The discovery was not accidental. It represented more than a style of rhetoric: it was an aesthetic and, above all, a world vision, a way of feeling, of knowing, and of expressing it.

This search for a modern and cosmopolitan tongue led the Spanish American poet, through a process apparently intricate but basically natural, to a rediscovery of the Hispanic tradition. I say *the*, not *a*, Spanish tradition because, unlike the tradition defended by the "purists," that discovered by the Modernists is the central and most ancient tradition of the language. And, precisely because of this fact, they could see it as that immemorial past that is also a perpetual beginning. Although it had been ignored by the traditionalists, that current was shown to be universal; it was the same principle[4] that ruled the work of the great Romantics and Symbolists: rhythm as the source of poetic creation and as the key to the universe. Thus it was not merely a question of restoration. As it recovered the Spanish tradition, Modernism added something new, something that had never existed before in that tradition. Modernism was a true beginning. Like French Symbolism, the Spanish American movement was a reaction against the vagueness and facility of the Romantics and at the same time our true Romanticism. The universe is a system of *correspondences*, ruled by rhythm; everything is coded, everything rhymes; every natural form says something, nature expresses itself in each of its changes; to be a poet is to be not the master but the agent of the transmission of rhythm; the highest form of imagination is the analogy. In all of Modernist poetry there is an echo of the Vers dorés: "Un mystère d'amour dans le métal repose; tout est sensible."

Nostalgia for cosmic oneness is a constant preoccupation of the Modernist poet, but he is also fascinated by the plurality in which that oneness manifests itself: "The celestial oneness that you presuppose," says Darío, "will cause diverse worlds to blossom within you." Dispersion of the being into forms, colors, and vibrations; fusion of all the senses into one. Poetic images are expressions, incarnations at once spiritual and

4. See note 3.—*Trans.*

sensual, of that plural and unique rhythm. This manner of seeing, hearing, and feeling the world is generally explained in psychological terms: synaesthesia. An exasperation of the nerves, an upheaval of the psyche. But it is something more: an experience in which the entire being participates. Poetry of sensations, it has been called; I would prefer poetry that, in spite of its exasperated individualism, affirms the world rather than the poet's soul. This explains the indifference, at times the open hostility, to Christianity. The world is not fallen, has not been abandoned by God. It is not a world of perdition: it is inhabited by the spirit; it is the source of poetic inspiration and the archetype of all happening: "Love your rhythm and make rhythm of your actions . . ." The poetry of the Spanish language had never before dared to affirm such a thing, had never seen nature as the dwelling place of the spirit, nor had it seen in rhythm the way, not to salvation, but to reconciliation between man and the cosmos. The libertarian passion of our Romantics, their rebellion against "the throne and the altar," are something very different from this vision of the universe in which there is so little place for Christian eschatology and in which the very figure of Christ is only *one* of the forms in which the Great Cycle manifests itself. The failure of our criticism to examine these beliefs is inexplicable. And, especially in Spain, that same criticism has accused the Modernist poets of superficiality! Modernism began as an aesthetic of rhythm and ended as a rhythmic vision of the universe. Thus it revealed one of the most ancient tendencies of the human psyche, covered up through centuries of Christianity and rationalism. Its revolution was a resurrection. A double discovery: it was the first appearance of the American sensibility in the arena of Hispanic literature; and it made Spanish verse the point of confluence between the ancestral background of American man and European poetry. At the same time it uncovered a buried world and re-created the ties between the Spanish tradition and the modern spirit. And one thing more: this Latin American poetic movement was impregnated with an idea foreign to the Spanish tradition: poetry is a revelation independent of religion. It is the original revelation, the true *beginning*. That is what modern poetry says, from Romanticism to Surrealism. In this vision of the world reside Modernism's originality and also its modernity.

Angel, specter, Medusa . . .
　　　Rubén Darío

Because of his age, Rubén Darío was the bridge from the initiators to the second Modernist generation; his travels and his generous activities made him the point of connection for the many scattered poets and groups on two continents; he not only inspired and captained the battle, he was also its spectator and its critic—its conscience; and the evolution of his poetry, from *Azul* [Blue] (1888) to *Poema del otoño y otros poemas* [Poem of autumn and other poems] (1910), corresponds to the evolution of the movement: it began with him and ended with him. But Darío's work did not end with Modernism: it surpassed it, went beyond the language of that school and, in fact, beyond that of any school. It is a creation, something that belongs more to the history of poetry than to the history of styles. Darío was not only the richest and most ample of the Modernist poets: he was also one of our great modern poets. He was the beginning. At times he makes one think of Poe; at other times, of Whitman. Of the first, in that portion of his work in which he scorns the world of the Americas and is preoccupied solely by an otherworldly music; of the second, in that portion in which he expresses his vitalist affirmation, his pantheism, and his belief that he was, in his own right, the bard of Latin America as Whitman was of Anglo-America. In contrast to Poe, Darío did not enclose himself within his own spiritual adventure; neither did he have Whitman's ingenuous faith in progress and brotherhood. More than to the two great North Americans, he could be compared to Hugo: eloquence, abundance, and that continuous surprise, that unending flow, of rhyme. Like the French poet's, his inspiration was that of the cyclopean sculptor; his stanzas are blocks of animated matter, veined with sudden delicacies: the striation of lightning on the stone. And the rhythm, the continuous swing that makes the language one enormous aquatic mass. Darío was less excessive and prophetic; he was also less valiant: he was not a rebel and he did not propose to write the Bible of the modern era. His genius was lyric, and he professed a horror of both miniaturism and titanism. More nervous, more anguished, he oscillated between contradictory impulses: one could say that he was a Hugo attacked by "decadent" ills. Despite the fact that he loved and imitated Verlaine above all (and above all others), his best poems have little resemblance to those of his model. He had superabundant health and energy; his sun was stronger, his wine more generous. Verlaine was a provincial Parisian; Darío a Central American globetrotter. His poetry is virile: skeleton, heart, sex. Clear and rotund even when it is sad; no halftones. His work, born at the very end of the century, is that of a Romantic who was also a Parnassian and a Symbolist. Parnassian: nostalgia for sculpture; Symbolist: prescience of analogy. A hybrid, not only because of the variety of spiritual influences, but also because of the bloods that flowed through his veins: Indian, Spanish, and a few drops of African. A rare being, a pre-Columbian idol, a hippogriff. In America, both the Anglo and our own, these graftings and superimpositions are frequent. America is one great appetite for *being* and, for that reason, a historical monster. Modern beauty and the most ancient beauty, are they not monstrous? Darío knew that better than anyone: he felt that he was a contemporary of both Moctezuma and Roosevelt-Nimrod.

He was born in Metapa, a small town in Nicaragua, on January 18, 1867. A few months after his birth his father abandoned the family home; his mother, whom he scarcely knew, left him to the care of an aunt and uncle. His real name was Félix Rubén García Sarmiento, but from the age of fourteen he signed himself Rubén Darío. A name like an unfolding horizon. Judea, Persia . . .[5] Precocity: innumerable poems, stories, and articles, all of them imitations of the literary currents in vogue. The civic themes of Spanish and Latin American Romanticism: progress, democracy, anticlericalism, independence, Central American union; and the lyric themes: love, the beyond, nature, Gothic and Arab legends. The erotic awakening was equally precocious: childhood love affairs, fascination with a Yankee trapeze artist, and, at fifteen, passion: Rosario Murillo. The attempt to marry her. His friends and family dissuaded him and sent him to El Salvador. There he made the friendship of Francisco Gavidia, who introduced him to the poetry of Hugo and of some of the Parnassians in the original. "Reading the alexandrines of the great Frenchman," he would later say, "inspired in me

5. In English, Rubén is Reuben, Darío is Darius.—*Trans.*

the ideas of metric renovation that I would later amplify and realize."
He still read French badly, but in some poems from those years, Anderson Imbert points out, there are indications of change: "In 'Serenata'
the hashish that Baudelaire and Gautier had introduced is now present
. . . and in 'Ecce Homo' there is spleen," the poetic sickness that was to
the nineteenth century what melancholy was to the seventeenth. In
1884 he returned to Nicaragua. A second encounter with Rosario
Murillo. His love had been violent and sensual, but only now did the
lovers achieve the final consummation. Darío discovered that Rosario
was not a virgin. Years later he would say that "an anatomical peculi-
arity made him suffer." Did not the deception hurt him more? Suffering, in 1886 he undertook his first great voyage: Chile. The great
periplus had begun. He would not stop traveling until his death.

In Santiago and Valparaíso he entered more civilized and more
restless worlds. It is not easy today to form an idea of what the Latin
American oligarchies were like at the end of the nineteenth century.
Peace had given them riches, and riches, luxury. If they had no
curiosity about what was going on in their own lands, they had a very
lively curiosity about what was occurring in the great cities overseas.
They did not create a civilization of their own, but they helped to refine
a sensitivity. In the personal library of his young friend Balmaceda,
Darío "quenched his thirst for new reading." Bohemia. Absinthe. The
first articles of combat: "I am with Gautier, the foremost stylist of
France!" He also admired Coppée and, above all, Mendès, his initiator
and guide. At the same time he continued writing washed-out imitations of the Spanish Romantics: now it was Bécquer and Campoamor.[6]
It was a farewell, since his aesthetic was now different: "The word must
paint the color of a sound, the perfume of a star, capture the soul of
things." In 1888 he published *Azul*. With that book, composed of stories
and poems, Modernism was officially born. The prose, especially, was
disconcerting, more daring than the poetry. In the second edition
(1890), Darío reestablished the balance with the publication of several

6. His first three books, written before he was twenty, constitute his con-
tribution to the reigning taste: *Epístolas y poemas* [Epistles and poems]
(1885), *Abrojos* [Thistles] (1887), and *Rimas* [Rhymes] (1887).

new poems: sonnets in alexandrines (an alexandrine never heard before in Spanish), others in different twelve-syllable lines, and another in a strange and rich meter of sixteen syllables. It was not only the unusual rhythms but also the brilliance of the words, the insolence of the tone, and the sensuality of the phrasing that irritated and bewitched. The title was almost a manifesto: was it an echo of Mallarmé ("Je suis hanté! L'azur, l'azur, l'azur, l'azur") or the crystallization of something that was in the air at the time? Max Henríquez Ureña points out that Manuel Gutiérrez Nájera had already demonstrated a similar fascination with colors. A spreading fan of preferences and paths to follow. In *Azul* there are five "medallions" in the manner of Heredia, dedicated to Leconte de Lisle, Mendès, Whitman, J. J. Palma, and Díaz Mirón; there is also a sonnet to Caupolicán, the first of a series of poems on "undiscovered America." All Darío: the French masters, Latin American contemporaries, pre-Hispanic civilizations, the shadow of the Yankee eagle ("The great old man lives in his iron country . . ."). In its time *Azul* was a prophetic book; today it is a historical relic. But there is one thing: a poem that is, for me, the first poem Darío wrote: I mean the first that is really a creation, a work. It is called "Venus." Every one of its lines is as sinuous and fluid as water seeking its path in the "profound extension" (because the night is not high, but deep). A black-and-white poem, a palpitating space in whose center opens the great sexual flower, "like a golden and divine jasmine inlaid in ebony." The final line is one of the most penetrating in our poetry: "Venus, from the abyss, looked at me with a sad gaze." Height becomes abyss and, from there, woman, fixed vertigo, watches us.

In 1889 Darío returned to Central America. A new encounter with Rosario Murillo. Flight to El Salvador, where he founded a daily newspaper championing Central American union, a cause to which he remained faithful all his life. He met Rafaela Contreras, the Stella of *Prosas profanas* [Profane hymns], and married her. Central American vagabonds: Guatemala, Costa Rica. In 1892 he went to Spain for two months. In the course of the voyage, on a stop at Havana, he met one of the first Modernists, Julián del Casal, and spent with him a memorable week of poetry, friendship, and alcohol. After his return from Spain, his wife died. She was in El Salvador while Darío was visiting Nicaragua. Psychic upheaval, alcoholism. In a short while, a relapse: Rosario Murillo. The passion became degraded: during one of his drunken sprees the brothers of his lover forced him to marry her, under threat of death. In 1893 he was named Colombian consul in Buenos Aires. Darío set out on the voyage, via New York and Paris, with Rosario, but he abandoned her in Panama. Not forever: that woman would pursue him with a kind of loving hatred until his death. In New York, another decisive meeting: José Martí. The stay in Paris was an initiation; on leaving, "he swore by the gods of the new Parnassus: he had seen the aged faun Verlaine, he knew the mystery of Mallarmé and was a friend of Moréas." In Buenos Aires he found what he had been searching for. Vivacity, cosmopolitanism, luxury. Between the pampas and the sea, between barbarism and the European mirage, Buenos Aires was a city more suspended in time than seated in space. Rootlessness but, at the same time, desire to invent itself, tension of creating its own present and its future tradition. The young writers had made the new aesthetic their own, and they crowded around Darío the moment he arrived. He was the indisputable leader. Years of agitation, polemics, and dissipation: the editorial room, the restaurant, the bar. Fervent friendships: Leopoldo Lugones, Ricardo Jaimes Freyre. Years of creation: *Los raros* and *Prosas profanas*, both in 1896. *Los raros* was the vade mecum of the new literature; *Prosas profanas* was and is the book that best defines the early Modernism: high noon, ne plus ultra of the movement. After *Prosas profanas* all openings closed: he must trim his sails or make the leap toward the unknown. Rubén Darío chose the former and reworked already known territory; Leopoldo Lugones risked the latter. Darío's *Cantos de vida y esperanza* [Songs of life and hope] (1905) and Lugones's *Lunario sentimental* [Sentimental almanac] (1909) are the two most important works of the second phase of Modernism, and from them derive, directly or indirectly, all the experiences and experiments of modern Spanish poetry.

   Prosas profanas: the title, halfway between erudite and sacrilegious, caused even more irritation than that of the earlier book. To call a collection of predominantly erotic poems *prosas*—hymns that are sung at High Mass, following the gospel—was more than an archaism, it was a challenge.[7] In addition, the title demonstrates a deliberate confusion between the vocabulary of the liturgy and that of pleasure. This persistent inclination, in Darío and other poets, is far from a caprice: it is one of the signs of the alternating fascination and repulsion that modern poetry experiences regarding traditional religion. The preface caused a scandal: it seemed to be written in another language, and everything it said sounded like paradox. Love of novelty, on condition that it not be of the present time; exaltation of the self and disdain for the majority; supremacy of the dream over the waking state and of art over reality; horror of progress, technology, and democracy ("If there is poetry in our America, it is in the ancient things, in Palenque and in Utatlán, in the legendary Indian, in the sensual and refined Inca, and in the great Moctezuma of the golden chair. The rest is yours, democratic Walt Whitman"); ambivalence, love, and mockery in regard to the Spanish past ("Grandfather, I must say it: my wife is from my country; my lover, from Paris"). Among all these declarations—clear-sighted or impertinent, ingenuous or affected—those of an aesthetic nature stand out. First: the freedom of art and its gratuitousness; second, the negation of all schools, not excluding his own: "My literature is mine, in me; whoever slavishly follows my footsteps will lose his own personal treasure"; and rhythm: "As each word has a soul, there is in every verse, in addition to its verbal harmony, an ideal melody. Music, many times, comes only from the idea."

Formerly he had said that things have souls; now he says that words also have them. Language is an animate world and verbal music is the music of souls (Mallarmé had written: of the Idea). If things have souls, the universe is sacred; its order is that of music and dance, a concert formed of the harmonies, joinings, and separations of one thing with another, of one spirit with others. To this idea, as ancient as man

7. Darío undoubtedly knew Mallarmé's poem "Prose pour des Esseintes," which appeared in 1885. Furthermore, his admiration for Huysmans is clear: "From September 1893 to February 1894," Max Henríquez Ureña says, "Darío wrote a column for a Buenos Aires newspaper under the pseudonym des Esseintes."

and always viewed with distrust by Christianity, modern poets add another: words have souls and the order of language is that of the universe: dance, harmony. Language is a magic double of the cosmos. Through poetry, language recovers its original being, becomes music again. Thus, ideal music does not mean the music of ideas but rather ideas that are in their essence music. Ideas in the Platonic sense, realities of realities. Ideal harmony: soul of the world; in its breast all things, all beings, are one same thing, one same soul. But language, although it is sacred by reason of participating in the musical animation of the universe, is also discord. Like man, it is contingency: the word is music and meaning at the same time. The distance between the name and the thing named, the meaning, is a consequence of the separation between man and the world. Language is the expression of consciousness of self, which is consciousness of the fall. Through the wound of meaning the whole being that is the poem bleeds and becomes prose: description and interpretation of the world. Despite the fact that Darío did not formulate his thought in exactly these terms, all his poetry and his attitude toward life reveal the tension of his spirit between the two extremes of the word: music and meaning. Through the first, the poet is "of the race that creates life with the Pythagorean numbers"; through the second, he has "the awareness of our human slime."

There was a certain incompatibility between the aesthetic of *Prosas profanas* and Darío's temperament. He was sensual, many-sided, gregarious, never reclusive: he knew and felt he was alone, but he was not a solitary person. He was a man lost in the worlds of the world, not an abstracted being gazing at himself. What gives unity to *Prosas profanas* is not its ideas but its feelings. Unity of tone, something very different from the spiritual unity that makes *Les fleurs du mal* [Flowers of evil] or *Leaves of Grass* self-sufficient worlds, works that unfold a single theme in vast concentric waves. The book of the Spanish American poet is a prodigious repertory of rhythms, forms, colors, and sensations. Not the history of an awareness but the metamorphosis of a sensibility. The metrical and verbal innovations of *Prosas profanas* dazzled and infected almost all the poets of those years. Later, through the fault of imitators and the fatal law of time, that style deteriorated and its music seemed cloying. But our judgment is different from that

of preceding generations. Certainly, *Prosas profanas* at times does recall an antique shop replete with Art Nouveau objects, with all its
splendors and rarities in questionable taste (and that now are beginning
to please us again). Alongside those trinkets, how can one help but
notice the powerful eroticism, the virile melancholy, the terror at the
pulsing of the world and one's own heart, the awareness of human
solitude when facing the solitude of things? Not everything in this book
is the rubbish of the collector. In addition to several perfect poems and
many unforgettable fragments, there is a grace and vitality in *Prosas
profanas* that still charm us. It is still a young book. They criticize its
artificialities and its affectations: have they noticed the exquisite and at
the same time direct tone of the phrasing, a knowing mixture of erudition and conversation? Solemnity and pathos had numbed the muscles
of Spanish poetry: with Rubén Darío, the language began to stride
again. His poetry was the prelude to contemporary poetry, direct,
spoken. It will soon be time to read that admirable and frivolous book
with new eyes. Admirable because there is no poem that does not contain at least one impeccable or disturbing line, the fatal vibration of
true poetry, music of this world, music of other worlds, always familiar
and always strange. Frivolous because its manner is close to mannerism
and its facility defeats its inspiration. Contortions, pirouettes: nothing
to criticize in those exercises if the poet had danced them on the edge
of the abyss. A book without abysses. And nevertheless . . .

Pleasure is the central theme of *Prosas profanas*. But pleasure, precisely because it is a game, is a rite from which sacrifice and pain are
not excluded. "Dandyism," said Baudelaire, "borders on stoicism." The
religion of pleasure is a rigorous religion. I would not reproach Darío
for the hedonism of *Prosas profanas*, rather for its superficiality. Aesthetic exigency is not converted into spiritual rigor. On the other hand,
passion glows in the best moments of the book, "black light that is more
light than white light." Woman fascinates him. She takes all natural
forms: hill, tiger, ivy, sea, dove; she dresses in water and fire, and, for
her, nudity itself is vestment. She is a font of images: in bed she "becomes a curled-up cat," and as she loosens her hair "two swans with
black necks" peer from beneath her blouse. She is the embodiment of
the "other" religion: "Somnambulist with the soul of Eloise, in her

there is the sacred frequency of the altar." She is the sensitive presence of that single and plural totality in which history and nature are fused:

> *. . . fatal, cosmopolitan,*
> *universal, immense, unique, one*
> *and all; mysterious and erudite;*
> *she—sea and cloud, spume and wave—loves me.*

Darío's eroticism is passionate. What he feels is perhaps not love for a single being but the attraction, in the astronomical sense of the word, of that incandescent star that is the apogee of all presences and their dissolution in black light. In his splendid "Coloquio de los centauros" [Colloquy of the centaurs], sensuality is transformed into passionate reflection: "All form is a gesture, a cipher, an enigma." The poet hears "the words of the mist," and the stones themselves speak to him. Venus, "queen of matrixes," rules in this universe of sexual hieroglyphics. She is All. Good and evil do not exist: "Neither is the wild pigeon benign, nor the crow perverse: they are forms of the enigma." Throughout his life Darío oscillated "between the cathedral and the pagan ruins," but his true religion was this blending of pantheism and doubt, exaltation and sadness, jubilation and fear. Poet of the astonishment of being.

The final poem of *Prosas profanas*, in my opinion the most beautiful in the book, is a résumé of his aesthetic and a prophecy of the future direction of his poetry. The themes of "Coloquio de los centauros" and other fine compositions here assume extraordinary density. The first line of the sonnet is a definition of his poetry: "I seek a form my style cannot discover." He seeks a beauty that is beyond beauty, that words can evoke but can never state. All of Romanticism—the desire to grasp the infinite—is in that line; and all of Symbolism—an ideal, indefinable beauty that can only be suggested. That form, more rhythm than body, is feminine. It is nature and it is woman:

> *The white peristyle is adorned with green palm trees;*
> *the stars have predicted that I shall see the goddess;*
> *and my soul reposes within the light, as the bird*
> *of the moon reposes upon the tranquil lake.*

It is scarcely necessary to point out that these superb alexandrines recall

those of "Delfica: Reconnais-tu le TEMPLE au péristyle immense . . ."
The same faith in the stars and the same atmosphere of orphic mystery.
Darío's lines evoke that "state of supernatural delirium" in which
Gérard de Nerval was said to have composed his sonnets. In the sestet
there is an abrupt change of tone. Doubt follows the certainty of the
vision:

> *and I find only the word that flies away,*
> *the melodious initiation that flows from the flute . . .*

A feeling of sterility and impotence—I was going to write, of in-
dignity—appears constantly in Darío, as in the other great poets of the
epoch, from Baudelaire to Mallarmé. It is the critical consciousness,
which at times resolves into irony and at others into silence. In the final
line the poet sees the world as an immense question: it is not man who
questions existence; it is existence that questions man. The line is
worth the whole poem, as the poem is worth the whole book: "And the
neck of the great white swan, that questions me."

In 1898 Darío made the great plunge. He was named correspondent
of *La Nación* [The nation], would live in Europe until 1914, and would
only return to his homeland to die. The life of a wanderer, divided
mainly between Paris and Mallorca. Newspaper assignments and diplo-
matic posts (consul general in Paris, minister plenipotentiary in
Madrid, delegate from Nicaragua to various international conferences).
Trips through Europe and America.[8] In 1900 he met Francisca Sánchez,

8. He visited our continent in 1906 (the Pan American Conference in Rio
de Janeiro), in 1907 (the famous trip to Nicaragua, which inspired a number of memorable poems), in 1910 (the interrupted trip to Mexico), and in
1912 (a round of conferences). Concerning the trip to Mexico: the interim
president of Nicaragua, Dr. José Madriz, had named him his representative
to the celebrations of the centennial of Mexican independence. While Darío
was on his way to Mexico City, Anglo-American troops occupied Nicaragua
and forced Madriz from power. To avoid international complications for
the Mexican government, the poet did not continue his trip to the capital.
In 1911 he published a political pamphlet about the Anglo-American inter-
vention in his country: "Refutation of President Taft."

the humble Spanish woman who was to accompany him on his European wanderings. It was devotion and loving pity, not passion. Those were the years of celebrity. Fame, good and bad: known as the central figure of our poetry, he was surrounded by the admiration of the best Spanish and Latin American poets (Jiménez, the two Machados, Valle-Inclán, Nervo), but he was also followed by a train of parasites, companions on unhappy sprees. Swift years, long hours in which he diluted his wine, his blood, in the "crystal cup of shadows." Creation and sterility, mental and physical excesses, the "futile search for happiness," the "false nocturnal blue" of drunkenness and "tearful sleep." Empty nights, examining his conscience in a hotel room: "Why does my soul tremble so?" But the wind in the deserted street, the murmur of advancing dawn, the mysterious and familiar sounds of an awakening city returned to him the old solar vision. During this period he published, in addition to many volumes of prose, his great books of poetry.[9] A good many of those compositions were a prolongation of an earlier phase, apart from the fact that some were written in the epoch of *Prosas profanas* and even earlier. But the more extensive and worthwhile portion reveals a new Darío, more serious and lucid, more whole and virile.

Although *Cantos de vida y esperanza* is his best book, the books that follow it continue in the same vein and contain poems that are equal to those of that collection. Thus, all these publications can be seen as a single book or, more exactly, as the uninterrupted flow of various simultaneous poetic currents. There is no break between *Prosas profanas* and *Cantos de vida y esperanza*. New themes appear, he expresses himself more soberly, more profoundly, but his love for the brilliant word does not diminish. Nor does his taste for rhythmic innovation disappear; on the contrary, these innovations are surer and more daring. Verbal

9. *Cantos de vida y esperanza* [Songs of life and hope] (1905), *Los cisnes y otros poemas* [The swans and other poems] (1905), *El canto errante* [The wandering song] (1907), *Poema del otoño y otros poemas* [Poem of autumn and other poems] (1910), *Canto a la Argentina y otros poemas* [Song to the Argentine and other poems] (1914). One must add the numerous works not collected in a volume until after his death.

plenitude, as much in the free verse as in those admirable re-creations of baroque rhetoric that comprise the sonnets of "Trébol" [Clover]: freedom, fluidity, continuous surprise of a language in perpetual movement, and, above all, communication between the written and the spoken language, as in the "Epístola" [Epistle] to the wife of Lugones, indisputable antecedent to what would be one of the conquests of contemporary poetry: the fusion of literary language and city speech. In sum, the originality of *Cantos de vida y esperanza* does not imply negation of the earlier period; it is a natural change, what Darío defines as "the profound work of an hour, the labor of a minute, and the prodigy of a year." Ambiguous portents, like those of the time.

The first poem in *Cantos de vida y esperanza* is a confession and a declaration. Defense of (and elegy for) his youth: "Was youth mine?"; exaltation and critique of his aesthetic: "The ivory tower tempted my desire"; revelation of the conflict that divides him and affirmation of his destiny as a poet: "Hunger for space and thirst for the heavens." The duality that manifests itself in *Prosas profanas* in aesthetic terms—the form that pursues and does not find its style—is now shown in its human truth: it is a schism of the soul. In order to express it, Darío uses images that burst almost spontaneously from what could be called his cosmology, if one understands by this not a system of thought but his instinctive vision of the universe. The sun and the sea rule the movement of his imagination; every time he looks for a symbol that defines the oscillations of his being, either aerial or aquatic space appears. To the first belong the heavens, light, stars, and, by analogy or sympathetic magic, the supersensitive half of the universe: the incorruptible and nameless region of ideas, music, numbers. The second is the domain of the blood, the heart, the sea, wine, woman, passions, and, also by magic contagion, the jungle, its animals and its monsters. Thus he compares his heart to a sponge saturated with the salt of the sea, and immediately after he compares it to a fountain in the center of a sacred jungle. That jungle is ideal or celestial: it is made not of trees but of harmony. It *is* harmony. Art extends a bridge between universes: the leaves and branches of the forest are transformed into musical instruments. Poetry is reconciliation, immersion in the "harmony of the great All." At the same time it is purification: "The soul that enters there should enter naked." For Darío poetry is practical or magical knowledge, a vision that is in itself a fusion of the cosmic duality. But there is no poetic creation without asceticism or spiritual combustion: "The star shines because of its nakedness." Darío's aesthetic is a kind of Orphism that does not exclude Christ (though it admits him as nostalgia rather than presence) or any of man's other vital and spiritual experiences. Poetry: totality and transfiguration.

A change of perspective corresponds to the change in the center of gravity. If the tone is deeper, the outlook is broader. History appears in its two forms: as living tradition and as struggle. *Prosas profanas* contains more than one allusion to Spain; the new books exalt it. Darío was never anti-Spanish, although the provincialism and conceit of Spain at the end of the century irritated him, as they did the majority of Latin Americans. But poetic renovation, at first received with distrust, had now conquered the young Spanish poets; at the same time, a new generation was initiating a rigorous and passionate examination of Spanish reality. Darío was not insensitive to this change, a change in which, incidentally, his influence had not been unimportant. And, lastly, his European experience had revealed to him the historical loneliness of the Spanish American. Divided by the harshness of geography and by the obtuse governments that prevailed in our countries, we were isolated from the world and also separated from our own history. This situation has scarcely changed today; and we know that the sensation of aloneness in space and time, the permanent basis of our being, becomes more painful outside our own countries. In the same way, contact with other Latin Americans, lost like us in the great modern cities, makes us immediately rediscover an identity that extends beyond the present artificial boundaries imposed by the combination of external power and internal oppression. Darío's generation was the first to be aware of this situation, and many of the Modernist writers and poets wrote passionate defenses of our civilization and attacks against imperialism. Darío abhorred politics, but the years of living in Europe, in a world indifferent to or disdainful of our own, caused him to turn his eyes toward Spain. He saw something more than the past in it, a still forceful element that gave unity to our disperseness. His vision of Spain was not exclusive: it embraced the pre-Columbian civilizations and the present of independence. Without either imperialist or colonialist nostalgia, the poet spoke with the same enthusiasm of the Incas, the conquistadors, and the heroes of our independence. He exalted the past but was distressed by Hispanic prostration, by the lethargy of our peoples, interrupted only by shudders of blind violence. He knew us to be weak and he looked with fear toward the north.

In those years, the United States, on the eve of becoming a world power, extended and consolidated its dominance in Latin America. In order to achieve this it used all measures—from Pan American diplomacy to the "big stick"—in a not infrequent mixture of cynicism and hypocrisy. Darío spoke out almost in spite of himself: "I am not a poet of the masses, but I know that unfailingly I must go to them." His anti-imperialism was not nurtured in the themes of political radicalism. He did not see the United States as the embodiment of capitalism nor did he conceive of the drama of Spanish America as a conflict of economic and social interests. The decisive element was the conflict between dissimilar civilizations in different historical periods: the United States was the youngest, most aggressive vanguard of a current—Nordic, Protestant, and pragmatic—in full ascent; our peoples, heirs of two ancient civilizations, were going through a period of decline. Darío did not close his eyes to Anglo-American greatness—he admired Poe, Whitman, and Emerson—but he refused to accept the possibility that that civilization was superior to our own. In the poem "To Roosevelt" he poses the progress-oriented optimism of the Yankees ("You think that . . . the future is wherever / your bullet strikes. No.") against a reality that is not of a material order: the Spanish American soul. It is not a dead soul: "It dreams, vibrates, loves." It is significant that none of these verbs designates political virtues: justice, liberty, energy. The Spanish American soul is a soul secluded in spheres that have little or nothing to do with human society: dreaming, loving, and vibrating are words that designate aesthetic, passional, and religious states. It was an attitude typical of the Modernist generation: José Enrique Rodó opposed Latin aesthetic idealism to Anglo-American pragmatism. These cursory definitions make us smile today. They seem superficial to us. And they are. But in them, in spite of their naïveté and the rhetorical presumption with which they were enunciated, there is something that modern ideologues do not suspect. The theme has a certain timeliness, and for that reason it does not seem entirely reprehensible to risk a digression here.

We have been accustomed to judging history as a struggle between antagonistic social systems; at the same time, because of our seeing civilizations as masks that cover true social reality—or as "ideologies," in the meaning that Marx gave to that word—we have come to attribute an absolute value to social and economic systems. A double error: on the one hand we specifically made ideology the historical value par excellence; on the other, we brought a gross Manichaeism upon ourselves. Today it again seems legitimate to think that civilizations, not excluding the mode of economic and technical production, are also an expression of a particular temper or, as one used to say, of the "genius" of a people. Perhaps "genius," because of its richness of associations, is not the most appropriate word: I will say that it is a matter of a collective disposition, more a consequence of a historical tradition than of a questionable racial or ethnic fatalism. The genius of a people would be that which shapes their social institutions and which, simultaneously, is shaped by them: not a supernatural power, but the concrete reality of a few men, in a determined landscape, with a similar heritage and a certain number of possibilities that may only be realized through, and thanks to, the action of the group. Finally, whatever may be our idea about civilizations, every day it seems more difficult to maintain that they are mere reflections, mere fantastic shadows: they are historical entities, realities as real as technical implements. Civilizations are the men that direct them. From this perspective the Sino-Soviet quarrel and the slow but inexorable dissolution of the Atlantic alliance take on another significance.

In theory, the enmity between Russians and Chinese is inexplicable, since this is a case of similar social systems that, by suppressing capitalism, have, again in theory, abolished economic rivalry, that is to say, the very root of political contention. Nevertheless, despite the fact that ideological dispute has neither economic nor social origins, it assumes the same form as struggles between capitalist nations.[10] For their part,

10. The *Communist Manifesto* says that antagonism between nations will disappear when the opposition of classes disappears.

the empirical "realists" assert that the quarrel about the interpretation of the texts, the "ideology," is actually a mask—except that it does not conceal economic or social realities but rather the ambition of rival groups fighting for hegemony. Is there not more to it? Can one avoid seeing in that conflict the clash of different manners of seeing and feeling? Can one ignore that some are Chinese and others Russian? The Chinese have been Chinese for more than three thousand years and it is not easy to believe that a quarter of a century of revolutionary government has erased millenniums of Confucianism and Taoism. The Russians are younger, but they are the heirs of Byzantium.

The same thing may be said about the difficulties that confront the Atlantic alliance. Incipient European unity has emphasized the fact that the affinities among the Europeans, from Spain to Poland, are greater and more profound than the ties that bind the United States and Great Britain to their continental allies. It is something that has little relation to the ruling social regimes. From the time of the Hundred Years' War the English have opposed all efforts toward European unification, whether they have come from the Left or the Right. And none of their political philosophers has really been interested in this idea. The United States has followed the same politics of separation, first in Latin America and later in the entire world. This policy is not the result of chance, nor is it only the reflection of a Machiavellian desire for universal domination. It is a historical style, the form in which a tradition and a sensibility are manifested. The Anglo-Saxons are a branch of western civilization that is defined above all by its desire for separation: they are ex-centric and peripheral. The Latin and Germanic traditions are centripetal; the Anglo-Saxon is centrifugal or, more accurately, pluralistic. Both tendencies have been in operation since the dissolution of the medieval world. They were not clearly visible during the apogee of nationalism because the turbulence of the struggle among the nation-states concealed them. Now that these states tend to group themselves into larger entities, the schism that has divided the western world since the Renaissance has surfaced: the pluralist tendency and the Roman-Germanic tradition. Although the Modernist generation ignored sociology and economics, it glimpsed the fact that conflict among civilizations cannot be reduced to a struggle for markets or a desire for power.

Nothing was more foreign to Darío than Manichaeism. He never believed that truths were exclusive, and he preferred to assume a contradiction rather than postulate anything that denied something else. He saw in Yankee imperialism the principal obstacle to the union of Spanish- and Portuguese-speaking countries. He was not mistaken. Neither was he mistaken in admiring the United States and in proposing its virtues to us as an example. The truth is that no Spanish American has dared to deny the existence and value of Anglo-Saxon civilization. On the other hand, Anglo-Americans have frequently denied ours. Our resentment against the United States is superficial: jealousy, a feeling of inferiority, and, above all, the irritation of one who is poor and weak who sees himself treated without equity. In Latin America there is no ill will toward Anglo-Americans. The true malevolence comes from them, and its root, in my opinion, is double: the feeling (unconfessed) of historical guilt and the envy (equally unconfessed) of forms of life that the pragmatic and puritanical conscience finds both immoral and desirable. For example, our concept of leisure fascinates and repels them and in both ways perturbs them: it calls their system of values into judgment. The psychic insecurity of the Anglo-Americans, when it does not erupt into violence, covers itself over with moralistic affirmations. This attitude causes them to discount or deny the questioner: they represent Good, and others, Error. Historical dialogue with them is particularly difficult because it always assumes the form of a judgment, a trial, or a contract. Our attitude toward Anglo-Americans is also ambivalent: we imitate them and we hate them. But we do not deny them. Although they have done and are doing us harm, we refuse to see them as a species different from our own, as the incarnation of evil. By tradition we are Catholic and liberal, and any exclusive vision of man, any form of puritanism, repels us. Rubén Darío shared the feelings of the greater part of Latin America. In addition, he was not a political thinker and his character was flexible: neither in public nor in private life was he a model of strictness. Hence it is not strange that in 1906, on attending the Pan American Conference at Rio de Janeiro as a delegate of his country, he wrote "Salutación al águila" [Greetings to the eagle]. This poem, which celebrates something more than collaboration between the two Americas, might make us doubt his sincerity. We would be unjust: he was honorable in his understandable and spontaneous enthusiasm. It did not last long. He himself confesses this in his "Epístola" to Lugones's wife: "In Rio de Janeiro . . . I panamericanized / with a vague fear and very little faith." Proof of his supreme indifference toward political consistency: both poems appeared, a few pages apart, in the same book.

In spite of these fluctuations, Darío continued to prophesy the resurrection of the Spanish American countries. Although he never said it clearly, he believed that, if the past had been Indian and Spanish, the future would be Argentine and, perhaps, Chilean. It never occurred to him to think that the unity and rebirth of our peoples could only be the result of a revolution that would overthrow the ruling regimes of his time and, with rare exceptions, our own. In *Canto a la Argentina y otros poemas* [Song to the Argentine and other poems] (1914) he combined his favorite ideas: peace, industry, cosmopolitanism, Latinity—the very gospel of the Spanish American oligarchies at the end of the century, with their faith in progress and in the superhuman virtues of European immigration. Not even a denunciation of revolutionary "aberration" is missing: "Anaké placed the bomb in the hand of Madness." The poem is a hymn to Buenos Aires, the coming Babel: "Concentration of Vedas, Bibles, and Korans." A single cosmopolis in the manner of New York, but "with a Latin perfume." The affairs of Latin America were not the only thing that inflamed him. He was in love with France ("The barbarians, dear Lutecia!"), and he was a burning pacifist. "Canto de esperanza" [Song of hope], a poem against war, contains a few marvelous lines, such as the first: "A great flight of crows stains the celestial blue . . ." The poem as a whole does not have the same vigor.

Darío's poetry of political and historical inspiration has aged as much as the decadent and the Versaillesque poems. If the decadent poems remind one of a curiosity shop, the political ones recall museums of national history: official glory, moth-eaten glory. If one compares these poems to those of Whitman, one immediately notices the difference. The Yankee poet does not write *about* history, he writes from it and with it: his words and Anglo-American history are one and the same thing. The poems of the Latin American are texts to be read from the rostrum before the audience at a civic celebration. There are moments, clearly, when the poet triumphs over the orator. For example, in the first part of "To Roosevelt," a model of insolence and of beautiful effrontery; some fragments of "Canto a la Argentina" [Song to the Argentine], where the verbal dexterity recalls Whitman—a Latin Whitman who has read Virgil; certain flashes of the visionary in the "Canto de esperanza" . . . It is not enough. Darío has little to say and he clothes this poverty in tinsel. He emits opinions, general ideas; he lacks Whitman's vision, a vision founded on what one sees, on reality, suffered and enjoyed. Darío's poems lack substance: terra firma, people. Substance: what lies below that sustains and nourishes us. Did he see the misery of our people; did he smell the blood of the slaughterhouse we call civil wars? Perhaps he tried to take in too much: the pre-Columbian past, Spain, the abject present, the radiant future. He forgot, or he did not wish to see, the other half: the oligarchies, oppression, the landscape of bones, broken crosses, and stained uniforms that make up Latin American history. He had enthusiasm; he lacked indignation.

All the work of Rubén Darío is bathed in a great sexual wave. He sees the world as duality, comprised of continuous opposition and copulation between masculine and feminine principles. The verb "love" is universal and to conjugate it is to practice the supreme science: it is not a knowledge of wisdom but of creation. But it would be futile to search for that passionate concentration that becomes an incandescent fixed point in his eroticism. His passion is disperse and tends to mingle with the fluctuation of the sea. In a very well known poem he confesses: "Plural has been the celestial / story of my heart." A strange adjective: if by "celestial" we mean that love that leads us to see in the loved one a reflection of the divine essence of the Idea, *his* passion does not easily respond to the qualifying word. Perhaps another acceptance of the word would be appropriate: his heart does not nourish itself from a vision of the motionless sky, but instead obeys the movement of the stars. The tradition of our love poetry, Provençal or Platonic, conceives of the loved one as reflected reality; the ultimate goal of love is not the carnal embrace, but contemplation, a prologue to the nuptials between the human soul and the spirit. That passion is a passion for unity. Darío aspires to the opposite: he wants to dissolve, body and soul, into the body and soul of the world. The story of his heart is plural in two senses: because of the number of women he loved and because of his fascination with the pluralism of the cosmos. For the Platonic poet the apprehension of reality is a gradual transition from the various to the one; love consists in the progressive disappearance of the apparent heterogeneity of the universe. Darío perceived this heterogeneity as the proof or manifestation of unity: every form is a complete world and, at the same time, is a part of totality. Unity is not one; it is a universe of universes, moved by erotic gravity: instinct, passion. Darío's eroticism is a magic vision of the world.

He loved several women. He was not what we call lucky in love. (What do we mean by that expression?) His misfortunes, if they really were that, do not explain the succession of love affairs or the substitution of one erotic object for another. Like almost all the poets of our tradition, he said he pursued a unique and single love: actually, he experienced perpetual vertigo before the plural totality. Neither celestial love nor fatal passion: neither Laura nor Jeanne Duval. His women were Woman and his Woman women. And more: female. His female archetypes were Eve and Venus. They "concentrate the mystery of the world's heart." Mystery, heart, world: feminine womb, primordial matrix. Sensual apprehension of reality: in woman "breathes the vital perfume of everything." That perfume is the opposite of essence: it is the odor of life itself. In the same poem Darío evokes an image that also seduced Novalis: the body of a woman is the body of the cosmos and loving is an act of sacred cannibalism. Sacramental bread, terrestrial host: to eat that bread is to appropriate the substance of life. Clay and ambrosia, the *flesh* of a woman, not her soul, is "celestial." This word designates, not the spiritual sphere, but vital energy, the divine breath that animates creation. A few lines later the image becomes more precise and daring: "Semen is sacred." For Darío the seminal liquid not only contains thought in its germinal form, it is also actually thought / matter. His cosmology culminates in an erotic mysticism: he makes of woman the supreme manifestation of plural reality, and he deifies semen.

The actors of this passion are not persons but vital forces. The poet does not seek to save his self or the self of his loved one: he seeks to dissolve them in the cosmic ocean. To love is to enlarge being. These ideas, common in the sexual alchemy of Taoism and of Hindu and Buddhist Tantrism, had never appeared with such violence in Spanish poetry, impregnated as it is with Christianity. (The sources of Spanish eroticism are different: Provençal poetry, Arabic mysticism, and the Platonic tradition of the Italian Renaissance.) Darío could not easily have been inspired by Oriental texts themselves, though no doubt he had vague notions about those philosophies. There is an echo of his Romantic and Symbolist readings in all this, but there is also something more: those visions are the fatal and spontaneous expressions of his sensitivity and his intuition. His originality consists in the fact that, almost without intending it, he revived an ancient manner of seeing and sensing reality. By rediscovering the solidarity between man and nature, the foundation of the earliest civilizations and the primordial religion of mankind, Darío opened a world of correspondences to and associations with our poetry. This vein of magic eroticism has been continued by various great Spanish American poets—by Pablo Neruda, for example.

Darío's imagination tended to manifest itself in contradictory and complementary directions, and therein lies his dynamism. The vision of woman as extension and as animal and sacred passivity—clay, ambrosia, earth, bread—is replaced by another: she is "the dark queen, a power whom the shadows fear." An active power: she dispenses good and evil with indifference. She embodies, one might say, the profound and sacred amorality of the cosmos. She is the siren, the beautiful monster, as much in the physical as the spiritual sense. All opposites come together in her: land and water, animal and human worlds, sexuality and music. She is the most complete form of the feminine half of the cosmos and in her song salvation and perdition are one and the same thing. Woman is anterior to Christ: she washes away all sins, she dissipates all fears, and her shining virtue is such that, "when she twists her locks, she quenches the fires of hell." Her attributes are double: she is water, but she is also blood. Eve and Salome:

And the head of John the Baptist,
who caused lions to tremble,
falls to the ax. Blood rains down.

But the sexual rose
as it opens
moves all that exists
with its carnal effluvium
and its spiritual enigma.

The archetypes of her universe are the womb and the phallus. They are present in all forms: "The hairy crab has rosy spines / and mollusks reminiscences of woman." The seduction of the second line comes not only from the rhythm but also from the conjunction of three distinct realities: mollusks, reminiscences, and women. Allusions to former lives are frequent in the poetry of Darío and imply that the chain of correspondences is also temporal. Analogy is the living web of which time and space are made: it is infinite and immortal. The enigmatic character of reality consists in the fact that every form is double and triple and that every being is a reminiscence or prefiguration of another being. Monsters occupy a privileged place in this world. They are the symbols, "clothed in beauty," of duality, the living signs of cosmic coupling: "The monster represents an anxiety in the world's heart." Darío's philosophy is resolved in this paradox: "to know how to be what you are, enigmas being forms." If everything is double and everything is animated, it is up to the poet to decipher the "confidences of the wind, the earth, and the sea." The poet is like a being without memory, like a child lost in a strange city: he does not know either where he comes from or where he is going. But this ignorance hides an unformed knowledge. Facing the Catalonian sea: "I feel in rock, oil, and wine / my own antiquity." The poet, a millennial child, is the awareness of the oblivion in which all human life is sustained: he knows we lost something in the beginning, but he does not know with certainty what it was that we lost or that lost us. He perceives "fragments of awareness of today and yesterday," he looks at the black sun, he weeps because he is alive, and he is astonished by his death.

The academic critic has generally preferred to close his eyes to the current of occultism that pervades Darío's work. This silence damages comprehension of his poetry. It is a question of a central current that constitutes a system of thought and also a system of poetic associations. It is his idea of the world or, rather, his image of the world. Like other modern creators who have used the same symbols, Darío transforms the "occult tradition" into vision and word. In a sonnet not collected in a volume during his lifetime, he confesses: "Pythagoras read the constellations, / I read the Pythagorean constellations." In the "confusion of his soul" his obsession with Pythagoras is mixed with his obsession with Orpheus, and both are mixed with the theme of the double. Duality now takes the form of personal conflict: who and what is he? He knows that he is "a felon, since the time of paradise"; he knows that he "stole fire and stole harmony," that he "is two inside himself," and that he "always wishes to be 'other.'" He knows that he is an enigma. And the answer to this enigma is another:

> *The golden turtle on the sand shows me*
> *where he conducts the chorus of the Muses*
> *and where the will of God augustly triumphs.*

In another sonnet, dedicated to Amado Nervo and also from his uncollected work, the golden turtle appears as the emblem of the universe. This composition seems to me to be one of the keys to the best- and the least-known Darío, and it merits a detailed analysis. Here I note only my perplexed fascination. The signs that the turtle traces on the ground and those that are drawn on its shell "tell us of the God without name." The form in which this unnamable divinity is revealed is that of a circle; that circle "holds the key to the enigma / that kills the Minotaur and astonishes Medusa." In the sonnet I first quoted, the turtle's teaching consists in showing the poet "the will of God"; in the one I mention now, that will is identified with eternal return. The divine work is the cyclic revolution that places what was down, up, and obliges everything to be transformed into its opposite: it immolates the Minotaur and petrifies Medusa. In the poet's spirit the signs of the turtle are converted into a "cluster of dreams" and a "bundle of flowering ideas." Union of the vegetable and mental worlds. This image is resolved in another, one of the poet's favorites: the signs are those of the music of the world. They are the emblem of cyclic movement and the secret of harmony: the orchestra and "what is suspended between the violin and the bow." A line swollen with divinations and reminiscences; a moment when the circular will, which perpetually begins again, pauses without pausing.

The analogy is imperfect. There is a flaw in the web of questions and replies: man. In "Augurios" [Auguries] the eagle, owl, dove, and nightingale fly over the poet's head, and each of those birds is an omen of strength, knowledge, or sensuality. Suddenly the enumeration changes direction, the symbolistic language breaks and erupts into direct speech: "A bat passes, / a fly, a horsefly . . ." Nothing passes, and death arrives. One is surprised by the bitter tone and the willful, dramatic prosaicness of the final lines. Dissolution of the dream into sordid quotidian death. The theme of our finiteness at times adopts Christian form. In "Spes" the poet asks Jesus, the "incomparable pardoner of wrongs," to resurrect him: "Tell me that this terrible horror of death / that obsesses me is but my heinous guilt." But Christ is only one of his gods, one of the forms of that God that has no name. Although rationalistic atheism was repugnant to Darío, and his temperament was religious—even superstitious—it cannot be said that he was a Christian poet, not even in the polemical sense that Unamuno was a Christian poet. Terror of death, horror of being, revulsion with himself—expressions that appear again and again following *Cantos de vida y esperanza*—are ideas and sentiments of Christian origin, but the other half, the Christian eschatology, is missing. Born into a Christian world, Darío lost his faith but, like the majority of us, kept the heritage of guilt—now with no connection to a supernatural sphere.

A feeling of original sin permeates many of his best poems: ignorance about our origin and our end, fear of the internal abyss, horror of living by feeling one's way. Nervous fatigue, exacerbated by a disordered life and alcoholic excesses, the coming and going from country to country, all contributed to his restlessness. He was living without a fixed course, scourged by anxiety; later he fell into lethargies that were "brutal nightmares" and he saw death alternately as either a bottomless well or a glorious awakening. Among these poems, written in a sober and reticent language, oscillating between monologue and confession, I am especially moved by the three nocturnes. It is not difficult to note the similarity to certain of Baudelaire's poems, such as "L'examen de minuit" [Midnight inquisition] or "Le gouffre" [The abyss].[11] The first and the last of the nocturnes end with the presentiment of death. He does not describe death, and he limits himself to naming it with the pronoun "She."[12] On the other hand, he feels that life is a bad dream, a mismatched collection of grotesque and terrible moments, laughable acts, unrealized projects, blemished emotions. It is the anguish of night in the city, its silence interrupted by "the clatter of a distant carriage" or the humming of the blood: prayer that changes to blasphemy, the endless reckoning of a man alone facing a future as closed to him as a wall. But everything resolves into serene joy if "She" appears. Darío's eroticism does not resign itself: it turns dying into a wedding.

In "Poema del otoño" [Poem of autumn], one of his last and greatest creations, the two currents that nourish his poetry join together: meditations on death and pantheistic eroticism. The poem is presented as variations upon the old and exhausted theme of the brevity of life, the flower of the instant, and other such commonplaces; at the end, the tone becomes graver and more defiant: in the face of death the poet affirms, not his own life, but that of the universe. Earth and sun vibrate within his skull as if it were a seashell; the salt of the sea, the vitality of sirens and tritons, mixes with his blood; to die is to live a greater and more powerful life. Did he really believe that? It is true that he feared death; it is also true that he loved and desired it. Death was his Medusa and his siren. Dualistic death, like everything else he touched, saw, and sang. Unity is always duple. That is why, as Juan Ramón Jiménez saw, his emblem is the seashell, silent but swelling with sounds, infinity that fits into one hand. It is a musical instrument that resounds with an "unknown accent"; a talisman that Europa has touched "with her divine hands"; an erotic amulet that convokes "the poet's beloved siren"; a ritual object whose hoarse music announces the dawn and the dusk, the hour in which light and shadow are joined. It is a symbol of universal correspondence. It is also a symbol of reminiscence: when he presses it to his ear he hears the surf of past lives. He walks along the sand, where

11. In the brief untitled poem that begins "O terremoto mental" ("O mental earthquake"), Darío directly quotes the French poet.

12. In Spanish, the word for death is feminine: *la muerte.—Trans.*

"the crabs leave the illegible scrawl of their claws," and his glance discovers the seashell: in its soul "another morning star like that of Venus is blazing." The seashell is his body and his poetry, the rhythmic fluctuation, the whirling of those images wherein the world is revealed and hidden, speaks and is silent. In the second nocturne he makes an accounting of what he lived and what he did not live, divided between "vast pain and petty cares," between memories and unhappiness, illuminations and violent joy:

> *All this has come in the midst of that boundless silence*
> *in which the night envelops earthly illusions,*
> *and I feel as if an echo of the world's heart*
> *had penetrated and disturbed my own.*

In 1914, with Europe at war, Darío returned to his native land. In addition to his physical and spiritual ailments, he was now suffering from financial difficulties. He conceived the idea of making a lecture tour throughout North America, assisted by a fellow countryman who was to serve as his business manager. He fell sick in New York and his companion deserted him. Mortally ill, he went to Guatemala. There the implacable Rosario Murillo gathered him up and took him to Nicaragua. He died in her house on February 6, 1916. "The seashell is in the shape of a heart." It was both his living breast and his dead skull.

L.K. & M.S.P.

José Juan Tablada

[NEW YORK, 1945]

The Mexican poet José Juan Tablada died on the second day of August 1945. He died here in New York,[1] in this city he loved so much, where he wrote some of his best chronicles, some of his most intense poems. It is barely a month since the poet died, but, when one looks back toward that August 2 of his death, one feels it was something that took place a long time ago. All of us, even the dead, grow older more quickly these days. This is not strange: we have been subjected to so many alternatives, so many diverse pressures, that time no longer flows at its normal speed. There are days that are months, months that are years. And this last month—the month of the atomic bomb, the Japanese surrender, and the universal peace—has been so full of public life that everything else, the living and dying of each day, has lost definition and can find no place, no space: universal history fills everything. How many events in just four weeks! And yet, as Charles Péguy said, "Homer is new each morning and there is nothing older than yesterday's newspaper." The news of Tablada's death can seem to us a distant fact, buried among other dates, and his death can grow dim, grow old, grow wrinkled like the wrinkled news in all the newspapers. But his poetry? Tablada's poetry has not grown old. It is not a news item but a fact of the spirit. And, when we read it, it seems as if the poet has not died and as if he had not written it many years ago. It is living, ironic, concentrated like a pungent herb, still resisting the years and the changing tastes of the day. It resists the news of his death. Each reader, if he reads it sympathetically, can relive the poems' adventures, can risk playing the game of the imagination that the smiling poet proposed. And if he reads with passion perhaps he will encounter new solutions to the old poetic enigmas, like the unexpected

1. These words were spoken at a meeting in homage to Tablada in New York, September 3, 1945.

find in a box of surprises. Because the work of José Juan Tablada is a little box of surprises, from which, in apparent disorder, come ostrich plumes, Modernist diamonds, Chinese ivories, little Aztec idols, Japanese prints, a sugar-candy skull, a pack of fortuneteller's cards, a drawing of "Fashion in 1900," a picture of Lupe Vélez when she danced at the Lyric Theater, a chandelier, a recipe by the nuns of San Gerónimo for hawthorn conserves, Arjuna's bow—fragments of cities, of landscapes, of skies, of seas, of epics. Each poem contains many riches, many joys, if the reader knows how to release the hidden spring. And we never know what the surprise awaiting us will be: the devil winking at us, a clown sticking out his tongue at us, or a rose that is a ballerina. Who knows into what colors the skyrocket will burst, and if its rain of fire will be green or yellow, when we see it climb the night sky during the fiesta?

Three poets—Tablada, Ramón López Velarde, and Enrique González Martínez—had considerable influence on the young people of their time. Each one represents a different effort, and their works show us the results of diverse experiences. González Martínez symbolizes classical prudence: he was born, as a poet, at the noonday of Modernism, and he interrogated it and grafted onto it a moral consciousness. González Martínez did not break with Modernist language: he lessened its excesses, he softened its highlights, but he used its own words to demonstrate its falsity. And thus, because he slowly eliminated the superfluous and exercised an intelligent taste when adopting any novelty, his work has been separating itself from the past, not in order to leap into the future, but rather to immobilize itself, severe and melancholic, like a noble statue in a garden in the outskirts. Unity and constancy—which are the virtues of serene rivers—give his work a navigable fluidity that never interrupts itself and never contradicts itself. López Velarde and Tablada, however, also deny Modernism in their language, not merely in their spirit. They represent curiosity, while González Martínez symbolizes moral meditation. But how different were the adventures of López Velarde and of Tablada! The poet from Zacatecas felt himself attracted to inner adventure, to the center of Mexico and the center of himself, whereas Tablada experienced the fascination of journeying, of flight: flight from himself and flight from Mexico. Journeys: a double

Paris, one seen through the eyes of Baudelaire and Symbolism, the other Dadaistic and Picassoesque; a Modernist Japan and another more profound and ascetic, where Basho converses with a tree and with himself; New York by day and by night; Bogotá, China, India, and a pyrotechnical Mexico. Journeys into space and journeys into time, journeys toward the past and toward the future, but, above all, journeys toward the present. His curious spirit was always lying in wait for what would arrive, always expecting the unexpected. His poetry tends toward imminence. This sensibility, so avid for temporal things, is perhaps the secret of the youthfulness of his work and is also one of its most obvious limitations. Tablada was always ready to board a train: he was a passenger poet, the poet of what is passing.

Tablada's prodigious trip to the world of poetry began from Modernism. All the excesses of language were taught in that literary dancing school. His poetry, wearing a black mask, crossed through the poetic carnival of the end of the century, adorned with supposedly rare gems and declaiming sumptuous sins. But he tired of the disguise, and as soon as Modernism became a vulgar fair he threw off his embroidered clothes. An attempt at nudity? No, a change of clothing. Not a trace of his Modernist past remained, except his fondness for words. (On the other hand, the footprints of Tablada's passage remain in the poetry of the Modernist period: some very characteristic poems, furniture for the museum of that epoch.) In 1919, when almost all the poets of the Spanish-speaking world were still thinking of poetry as an exercise in amplification, he published a small book from his exile in Caracas: *Un día* [A day], synthetic poems. Then, in 1922, in New York, another: *El jarro de flores* [The jar of flowers]. These were made up of three-line poems in which, more than capturing a feeling or an object, the poet opened a window onto an unknown perspective. With these two books Tablada introduced the Japanese haiku into the Spanish language. His innovation was something more than a mere literary importation. That form gave images their liberty and rescued them from anecdotal poetry, in which they were suffocating. Each one of those little poems was a small, wandering star and, almost always, a small, self-sufficient world. Years later, other poets discovered the value of an image isolated from rhyme and from the logic of the poem; but, while to them each image was an arrow shot at an unknown target or a loose bead of a necklace, to Tablada each image was a poem in itself and each poem a world of unforeseen relationships, at once profound and limpid. When he sketches a monkey in three lines—

> *The little monkey looks at me:*
> *he wants to tell me something,*
> *but he forgets what it is.*

—is it not true that we feel a chill? In those three lines Tablada has hinted at the possibility that it is the monkey who recognizes himself in us, that it is he—and not the man—who remembers his past. The same inquietude, made up of pleasure and perplexity, overcomes us when we reread "Insomnia":

> *It adds up phosphorus numbers*
> *on a black blackboard.*

There is no need to say more. It is not that everything has been said: the poet has merely opened a door and invited us to go in. As in those Japanese drawings in which the trembling of a line seems to capture the echo of the wind's passing, Tablada offers us a liquid green landscape when he sketches a tree:

> *Tender willow,*
> *almost gold, almost amber,*
> *almost sunlight.*

Tablada's haikus had many imitators. There was a whole school, a whole manner, that has lasted until today. Perhaps its true importance does not reside in those echoes but rather in this: Tablada's experiences contributed toward making us aware of the value of images and the power of concentration in language.

In 1920, also in New York, he published a new book called *Li-Po*, made up of ideographic poems. The poet kept up with his times and almost got ahead of them: French poets were continuing the games and experiments initiated by Apollinaire, and Imagist poetry was triumphing in the English language. Tablada was indebted to both groups, and what he gathered from the two currents was not a servile imitation but rather a delight in poetic typography and archaeology (versions of Chinese and Japanese poetry, worlds that had already interested him during his Modernist youth). There is an ingenious poem in *Li-Po* that is a small masterpiece, a poetic game with conflicting images and a final collision, something that has very rarely been tried in our poetry:

ALTERNATING NOCTURNE

Golden New York night
   Cold Moorish stucco walls
Rector's champagne fox trot
   Mute houses and stout grilles
And the soul looking backward
   The white cats of the moon
Stands petrified
   On the silent rooftops
Like Lot's wife
   And yet
     in New York
     and Bogotá
      the moon
       is one
        and the same!

These changes were not mere pirouettes but rather the expressions of an always curious and insatiable spirit. He was the Don Juan of poetry, and each adventure stimulated him to a new escape and a new experience. His tastes changed, but not his object: he was not enamored of this or that kind of poetics but with poetry itself. Since he was gifted with fantasy and an unquenchable aesthetic enthusiasm—which can also be seen in his chronicles and art criticism—nothing new was alien to him. "The pyramids are the pharaohs' sleeping caps," he wrote in a preface in 1918. He defined himself in this way: "Everything depends on the concept one has of art; there are those who believe it to be static and definitive; I believe it to be in perpetual motion. A work of art moves toward itself, like a planet, and around the sun." And, moving toward himself, around the sun in the orbit of López Velarde, he finally returned to Mexico years later. The Mexico he then discovered was not the Frenchified country it had been under Porfirio Díaz but the real Mexico that had been rescued by the Revolution, by its musicians and painters, and, above all, by López Velarde. Tablada generously acknowledged this in his "Retablo" [Retable]:

> *Poet of town and countryside,*
> *your Poetry was the miraculous*
> *Apparition on the barren Peñón*[2]
> *in a nimbus of roses and stars,*
> *and today our souls walk in your footprints*
> *to the provinces, on pilgrimage.*

The Mexico of *La feria* [The fair] (New York, 1928) is not intimate and somnambulistic like that of López Velarde; it is external and decorative. A Mexico of noise and color, baroque and popular, of the fifteenth of September[3] and the Christmas piñata. An Indian and mestizo Mexico, masked like an Aztec priest, delirious like the drunkard and the skyrocket, those uproarious twins. A Mexico of the ballet. The poet sings to the somber, ecclesiastical *mole*,[4] to the joy of "golden chickens among green lettuces," to the parrot that "is only a sprig of foliage with a bit of sun for a topknot," to the song of the rooster that "flings to the sky the coins of the seven of *oros*,"[5] to the idol in the churchyard, to the bells in the tower, to the kite, to everything in Mexico that dances or leaps, howls or sings, spins or glitters. But he is not blinded by the confusion of colors or deafened by the songs and shouts; he is able to

2. The hill at Tepeyac where Our Lady of Guadalupe, the patroness of Mexico, appeared to the Indian Juan Diego.—*Trans.*

3. Mexico's Independence Day.—*Trans.*

4. A sauce made of chiles and other ingredients; *mole poblano* is a dark, red brown *mole* said to have been invented by nuns in the city of Puebla.— *Trans.*

5. A suit, represented by gold coins, in a deck of Spanish playing cards.— *Trans.*

hear the silence of the central plateau and to perceive in that silence
the mystery of the ancient mythologies:

> *There is a rock*
> *in the middle of the field*
> *that is taking the shape*
> *of the great warlock Tezcatlipoca.*[6]

In homage to the Mexican Revolution, Tablada engraves this little drypoint:

> *The moon writes "Human justice"*
> *on the marshland pools*
> *with a quicksilver crayon,*
> *and a corpse clutches in each hand*
> *an ear of corn.*

He is criticized for a lack of unity that he never sought. In him, unity
resides in his fidelity to the adventure. Instead, why not look at the
other virtues of his poetry: curiosity, irony, power of concentration,
agility, renewed freshness of imagery. And how can we forget that
this poet, whom everyone judges to be so affected and literary, was the
only one among us, until the appearance of Carlos Pellicer, who dared
to look at nature with clear eyes, without changing it into symbols
or decorations? His infinite feelings of sympathy with animals, trees,
plants, or the moon led him to discover the old door that had been
sealed away for centuries: the door that opened communication with
the instant. At its best moments Tablada's poetry is a miraculous agreement with the world. Are we so insensitive to true poetry that we ignore
the poet who has had the liveliest and purest eyes of this epoch and
who has shown us that the word is capable of reconciling man with
the stars, and animals, and roots? Tablada's work invites us to life. Not
to the heroic life, not to the aesthetic life, but simply and only to life.
And to adventures and to journeys. He invites us to keep our eyes open,

6. Smoking Mirror, one of the chief gods of the Aztec pantheon, with
protean attributes.—*Trans.*

to learn how to quit the city where we were born and the kind of poetry that has become a bad habit; he invites us to seek out new skies and new loves. "Everything is in motion," he tells us, "in motion toward itself." And, as we now know, to return toward ourselves we must first go out and take risks.

L.K.

The Road of Passion

1. A SCRUPULOUS BALANCE

*The ordinary meaning of language has been lost to us, and
the dictionary whispers . . .*
                                        Ramón López Velarde

Reading the book that Allen W. Phillips devoted to Ramón López
Velarde led me to reflect once again on the case of this poet.[1]
The first surprising thing is his literary fortune. After an initial
period of public incomprehension, his poetry, sparse and difficult, has achieved a renown and a permanence that larger and more
accessible bodies of work have not attained. In his lifetime López
Velarde published only two books of poems: *La sangre devota* [Devout
blood] (1916) and *Zozobra* [Anxiety] (1919). Three volumes were
published after his death, one of poetry, *El son del corazón* [The sound
of the heart] (1932), and two of prose, *El minutero* [The minute hand]
(1923) and *El don de febrero* [February's gift] (1952); there are, in
addition, several unpublished poems and articles and some short stories.
Does what he left really constitute an oeuvre? In my opinion, what he
wrote before 1915 does little to substantiate such a premise. And I believe, contrary to the opinion of many, that his premature death interrupted his work precisely at the moment when he was moving toward
a loving contemplation of reality, less intense, perhaps, but fuller than
the concentrated poetry of his principal book, *Zozobra*. At the same
time, López Velarde left us a few poems in verse and prose—fewer than
thirty—so perfect that it is foolish to lament those that death prevented
him from writing. That handful of texts provokes a number of questions

1. Allen W. Phillips, *Ramón López Velarde: El poeta y el prosista* (Mexico City, 1962).

in every attentive reader. For more than thirty years there has been a great effort to answer them critically: López Velarde, a provincial poet, a Catholic poet, a poet of eroticism and death, even a poet of the Revolution. And there are other questions, more decisive than the purely literary ones. I resolved, once again, to question those poems the way one questions oneself. The pages that follow are my response. But first I must say something about the book that motivated me to write about López Velarde again.

I believe that Phillips's study is the most complete that has been written about our poet. It is an intelligent résumé: by that I mean it is a critical interpretation of everything that has been said on the theme; at the same time, it is a true exploration of a singularly complex body of work. In my judgment, there are three important moments in the history of López Velarde criticism: the essay by Xavier Villaurrutia that literally disinterred a great poet who had been buried beneath the rubbish of anecdote and facile enthusiasm; some valuable studies on particular aspects of his life and work, among which those by Luis Noyola Vázquez are outstanding; and this book by the North American critic, which finally offers us the possibility of a more definitive understanding. I was especially interested in the chapters on López Velarde's formative years. I believe that in his time no one except José Juan Tablada entirely realized the meaning of López Velarde's experiment. Although critics persist in disdaining the influence of Tablada's poetry, as well as its worth, Tablada served as a stimulus and an example for López Velarde.[2] With this one exception our poet lived his literary life

2. The letters between Tablada and López Velarde, around 1919, on the subject of Apollinaire are a curious testimony to this. Apollinaire's *Calligrammes* appeared in 1918, but the first poem-ideogram—as he called those compositions—"Lettre-océan," was published in 1914. Written (should I say drawn?) on a post card of the Mexican republic, it contains various picturesque allusions to our country and is dedicated to his brother, Albert Kostrowitzky, who lived in Mexico from 1913 until his death in 1919, never having returned to France. José M. González de Mendoza enjoyed a friendship with him. They frequented the YMCA gymnasium and sometimes talked about poetry. One day González ran into Kostrowitzky on Balderas

amidst the reserve of the Ateneo[3]—whose members similarly showed no enthusiasm for Tablada—and the cordial but limited devotion of the companions of his generation. Shortly before his death the young men who would later join together on the journal *Contemporáneos* [Contemporaries] discovered in him, if not a guide, a kindred spirit, another solitary. And years later one of them, Xavier Villaurrutia, wrote an essay about López Velarde's work that for its strict geometry and its broad and profound rhythm is reminiscent of certain of Baudelaire's texts.

Phillips's book says almost everything there is to say about the influence of Spanish and Spanish American poets on López Velarde. The North American critic perceives echoes of Darío's nocturnes from *Cantos de vida y esperanza* [Songs of love and hope] in certain poems from *La sangre devota*. This observation is accurate, and it helps us define López Velarde's poetic lineage. I would add something further: perhaps one should read the forgotten Efrén Rebolledo again; some of his erotic sonnets are vaguely reminiscent of poems in *Zozobra*. As for López Velarde's reading French poets, perhaps it would be well to consult the first edition of the anthology by Enrique Díez-Canedo and Fernando Fortún. Surely López Velarde was familiar with it. Some years ago Pablo Neruda confided to me that he owed his first contact with French poetry to that book—emphatically adding, "like almost all Spanish American poets of that time." I do not agree with the paragraphs that Phillips devotes to Francis Jammes; it is evident that López Velarde profited from this poet's lesson, but his influence is undeniably superficial. True influence, in my opinion, acts as fertilization or illumination; it is born of an encounter and is the result of spiritual affinity. The influence of Rodenbach, and especially of Verhaeren and Maeterlinck, seems even more dubious to me. Very simply, those names were a part of the artistic and intellectual atmosphere of the day. These

---

Street, who showed him a telegram from Paris and said, "My brother died yesterday. He was the best poet in France, although few people knew it . . ."

3. The Ateneo de la Juventud ("athenaeum of the young") was formed in 1909 by a group of intellectuals and writers.—*Trans.*

small observations do not detract from the fact that Phillips's study confirms something that has not been emphasized enough: French literature is a much more determining factor on López Velarde than it would seem at first glance.

The subject of the relationships between Baudelaire and our poet is essential to a study of his work. Here, too, I do not entirely agree with Phillips. In an article I wrote about López Velarde in 1950, I questioned the similarity between Baudelaire and López Velarde that Villaurrutia argued with such subtlety. I would not do the same today. In that article I emphasized the differences between the two. The "abyss," to use Villaurrutia's expression, that attracts Baudelaire is that of a self-sufficient but at the same time helpless consciousness—hence the identification of evil with human liberty and of both qualities with nothingness. López Velarde, on the other hand, feels the fascination of the flesh, which is always a fascination with death: as he sees "the furrow sex leaves in the sand," the world becomes "an impassioned mausoleum." The vision of the body as both an adorable presence and something condemned to putrefaction approximates, but is not identical to, the spiritual vertigo that zealously seeks "the insensibility of nothingness." But these differences should not blind us to the poets' many profound similarities. Both are "Catholic poets," not in the militant or dogmatic sense, but in their anguished relationship, alternately rebellious and dependent, with traditional faith. The eroticism of both is tinged with a cruelty that turns back upon them: to "Je suis la plaie et le couteau" ("I am the wound and the knife") the Mexican responds with "ser en un solo acto el flechador y la víctima" ("to be in one single act the archer and the victim"). Both love spectacles of funereal luxury: the courtesan—incarnation of time and death—ballerinas, clowns, female animal tamers, marginal human beings, images of grandeur and misery. In both there is the same continuous oscillation between sordid reality and ideal life ("edén provinciano" ["provincial Eden"] and "chambre spirituelle" ["spiritual bedchamber"]): idolatry of the body and horror of the body, systematic and conscious confusion between religious and erotic language, not in the natural manner of the mystics but with a kind of blasphemous exasperation . . . In a word, there is the same love of *sacrilege*.

Baudelaire has an incomparably richer and profounder spirit, but López Velarde is of his kind. To prove it one has only to compare some prose poems from *El minutero*—among others, "José de Arimatea," "El bailarín" [The dancer], "Obra maestra" [Masterpiece]—with certain texts from *Le spleen de Paris* [The spleen of Paris]—for example, "L'horloge" [The clock], "La chambre double" [Room for two], and "Mademoiselle Bistouri." Need I continue? And we have López Velarde's confession: "Seminary student, without Baudelaire, no sense of smell, no sense of rhyme." Here Phillips cites an unfortunate interpretation by Bernardo Ortiz de Montellano ("here the sense of smell means malice") that had provoked the reasoned indignation of Villaurrutia. Actually, besides the fact that Montellano forgot that every poetic word contains a multitude of meanings, López Velarde's poetry itself stirs up a sea swell of heavy and intense perfumes, a vibration prolonged in resonances that I feel inclined to call spiritual: incense, the odor of damp earth and lilies, clay, orange blossom, musk, aromas of bedchamber and church, bed and cemetery . . . The catalogue is impressive not only for the number of sensations but also for their complexity. And in the center of that sensual constellation, like a staring eye, is the name of Baudelaire: the sacrilegious consciousness.

It seems clear to me that the affinities between López Velarde and Laforgue cannot be denied. I continue to believe everything I said about this in my article in 1950. Whether read in French, in translation, or through the intermediary figure of Lugones, Laforgue's poetry is central to López Velarde's work. The French poet revealed to him the secret of the fusion between the language of prose and the poetic image or, if you will, the formula for the ice and incandescence of the word. Not the opposition between everyday life and poetry, but their mingling: absurd situations, oblique revelations, theatrical asides, the alliance of the grotesque, the tender, and the delirious. The moon and the cold shower. Above all, Laforgue showed him how to stand apart from himself and to observe himself without self-complicity: the monologue, the doubling of the "I" who speaks in the "I" who listens. The monologue, the face that contemplates itself in the convex mirror of irony, introduces the use of prose as an essential element of the poem. But one must not confuse this use of prose with the employment of what we call popular or folkloric language. About that time in Spain, Machado was attempting to return to the speech of the people, and later, although within an aesthetic closer to that of Jiménez, García Lorca and Alberti also attempted it. Whatever our opinion of these poets, I do not believe that anything resembling popular language can be found in their poems. It is not difficult to ascertain why: their language is more nearly a vague philosophic notion inherited from Herder and German Romanticism and has little real substance.

The so-called popular language of Spanish poetry does not come from the language of the people, rather from the traditional song, whereas the language of López Velarde and of other Spanish American poets derives from conversation, that is, from the language actually spoken in cities. For this reason, it permits the use of technical terminology, neologisms, and local and foreign words. Whereas traditional songs are nostalgia for another time, poetry in the colloquial vein brings the idiom of the past face to face with that of today and thus creates a new language. One accentuates lyricism, the other tends to break it: the function of this new language within the poem is the criticism of poetry. One cannot improve upon what López Velarde says: "The poetic system has been converted into a system of criticism." Somnambulism and examination of consciousness. Time, that famous temporality, is abysmal and discontinuous. Song recovers it, like the clock that hides real time from us as it measures the hours. Song carries us to other times; the poem that López Velarde attempted opens consciousness to real time. A violent operation, since man, who lives in time and who perhaps is nothing but time, closes his eyes and wishes never to see time, wishes never to see himself.

The favorite form of both Laforgue and López Velarde was the poem whose sinuous lines imitate the zigzag progress of the monologue: confession, exaltation, brusque interruption, marginal commentary, leaps and lapses of the word and spirit. The monologue is time: song and prose. For that reason it does not accommodate itself to the traditional lyric with its fixed meters and ready rhymes; it prefers free verse and unexpected rhyme. Irony is its bridle and the adjective its spur. Even more notably than Laforgue—and following Lugones, whom he repeatedly compared to Góngora—our poet proposed that each of his poems be a "psychological equation" and a sensual organism, a hybrid object.

I want to repeat here that Lugones's influence on López Velarde was decisive. The language of *Lunario sentimental* [Sentimental almanac], in the broadest and most radical meaning of the word "language," is one of the keys to López Velarde's style. Thanks to Lugones he discovered himself; but no sooner did he find himself than he ceased to resemble the great Argentine poet. Phillips observes with precision: "The burlesque and the cunning, the festive and the picturesque, the exuberant and the merry, predominate in Lugones. . . . In Laforgue and López Velarde the attitude is more profound: both conceal an inherent sadness beneath their mask of irony." I would add that in Lugones there is not that moral dimension—a heritage from Baudelaire —that is consciousness of self; neither is there the sensation of loneliness in the urban multitude nor, finally, a sense of the supernatural. Lugones could never have written the following sentence by López Velarde, which Laforgue would have signed and which is, simultaneously, the key to López Velarde's style and a self-definition: "The lost steps of consciousness, the falling of a glove in a metaphysical well . . ." In these lines there is a presentiment of something he never saw: Chirico's paintings. And other things. So, although the affinity between the Frenchman and the Mexican is greater than that between the two Spanish Americans, Laforgue is more dry and intellectual: there is a mundane rictus in his smile that reveals a withered soul. López Velarde is more ingenuous, serious, and virile; he mocks himself, but he does not deny either poetry or love. And something decisive separates them: the religiosity that is alive in one, dead in the other.

It seems important here to locate López Velarde not merely within the area of Mexican poetry, as is the restrictive custom, but also within the larger area of Latin American and (and why not?) universal literature. At that period the young Vicente Huidobro, in Santiago or in Paris, was preparing an eruption that was to disconcert and irritate, among others, Antonio Machado. In Mexico (or, more exactly, in Bogotá) Tablada was writing *Un día* [A day], a slim book that López Velarde regarded as perfect, a book our criticism still has not digested. And what was happening on the rest of the continent and on the

Spanish peninsula? In order to find anything equivalent to López Velarde's adventure, we must go to the English language. Pound published *Lustra* in 1916 and *Hugh Selwyn Mauberley* in 1920; and those were also the years of T. S. Eliot's initiation. There is a certain similarity between the early Eliot (up to "The Love Song of J. Alfred Prufrock") and the late López Velarde. It is a question, of course, of a distant relationship; both have common ancestors. This resemblance is short-lived (it could be said that Eliot begins where López Velarde leaves off), but it reveals how superficial it is to confine our poet within the framework of the provinces. His work is contemporary with his time in spite of the historical and geographical distance at which he lived. No, López Velarde is not a provincial poet, although his homeland is one of his themes. The provincial ones are the majority of those who criticize him. Such poems as "El mendigo" [The beggar], "Todo" [All], "Hormigas" [Ants], "Tierra mojada" [Damp earth], "El candil" [The lamp], "La última odalisca" [The last odalisque], and others—in verse and in prose—make him a modern poet, something that could not be said of almost any of his Spanish-language contemporaries in 1916 or 1917.

It must be repeated: modern poetry was born in Spanish America before it was born in Spain (with the one great exception of Gómez de la Serna), and one of its initiators was López Velarde. With him began a *vision* that continues to seduce spirits as diverse as Jorge Luis Borges and Pablo Neruda. The gaze that gazes on itself, the knowing that knows it knows, this vision is the attribute (the condemnation would be more accurate) of the modern poet. López Velarde lived in a complex moral situation—and he knew he was living in it, to the extent that the knowing became more real than lived reality. In an article he said: "He who is not capable of taking his own pulse will not go beyond scribbling trivial prose and empty verses." Aware of his own fatality, and aware of that awareness: from thence spring irony and prosaism, the violence of the blood and the perfidious artifice of the adjective. A mortal game of reflections: the transparency of the word opposed to the opacity of things, the transparency of the consciousness opposed to the opacity of words, and the infinite reflection of one word in another, of one consciousness in another. This conflict has a name: multiplicity. The consciousness wanders lost among the disperseness of objects, souls, and female bodies. Woman is the key to the world, the presence that reconciles and binds together disjoined realities; but she is the presence that multiplies itself and thus denies itself in infinite presences, all of them mortal. Feminine multiplicity: duplicity of death. Time and time again the poet attempts to reduce this disperseness to unity. Time and time again woman is converted into women and the poem into fragment. Unity offers itself only in death or in the solitary consciousness. Poetry of a solitary man for solitary men.

López Velarde's style, concentrated and complex, is triumphant in its fixed intensity: that moment when the blood rushes, when thought is suspended or the spirit enraptured. That instant of frenzy that reaches a peak, becomes immobilized, and then is obliterated. Aesthetic of the heart and its beating. And, also, a style of excesses—not exterior, but interior. Its temptation is not external immensity but the infinitesimal; and its danger is not pompous vagueness but tortured affectation. Many of López Velarde's sentences give us the sensation not so much of perfection as of tortured language. One must confess that López Velarde frequently is labored, sometimes even tasteless. In my opinion, a considerable portion of his youthful writing, in prose and in verse, is sentimental, artificial, and, frankly, unbearable. His taste was demanding but not impeccable. The literary atmosphere of those days was contaminated by the death throes of Modernism, whose followers had degraded its rhetoric into a side show of stereotyped curiosities. Even Jiménez did not free himself of that contagion until years later. López Velarde never completely abandoned some of the peculiarities of his earlier poetry. Gorostiza suggests that his provincialism could explain some of his affectations. Whatever the origin of his attitude, the essential newness of his imagination was more powerful than his equivocations in taste.

A concentrated and complex poet with a meager body of work. To this description another quality must be added: he was limited. His themes are few, his spiritual interests narrow. There is no sense of history in his work. When I say history, I am referring to general or universal history. There is no other: what one calls the history of one's homeland is either the mirror of man—and thus also universal—or merely an after-dinner anecdote. Neither was he aware of knowledge and all its drama: López Velarde never questioned the reality of the world or of man, and it would never have occurred to him to write *Muerte sin fin* [Death without end] or *Ifigenia cruel* [Cruel Iphigenia]. The relationships between wakefulness and dream, language and thought, consciousness and reality—the constant themes of modern poetry since German Romanticism—seldom figure among his preoccupations. He seated "beauty upon his knee," but did he "find her bitter"? At any rate, he did not damn her. He did not blaspheme, did not prophesy. He did not aspire to godhead, nor did he feel any nostalgia for the animal state. He neither adored the machine nor sought the golden age among the Zulus, the Tarahumaras, or the Tibetans. With the exception of one poem of beautiful violence ("Mi corazón leal, se amerita . . ." [My loyal heart deserves . . .]), he was not moved to rebel. He did not, through his poetry, wish to change man or transform the world. Insensitive to the murmur of the future arising in those years throughout the confines of the planet, insensitive to the great spaces opening to the spirit, insensitive to the very planet emerging for the first time in history as a total reality . . . did he suspect that modern man, for more than a hundred years, has been torn between utopia and nihilism? Worries that kept Marx, Nietzsche, and Dostoevsky awake at night did not spoil his sleep. In short, he was removed from almost everything that agitates us today. It is paradoxical that a spirit so impervious to the anguishes, desires, and fears that others feel could have been converted into that equivocal figure designated by the phrase "national poet." I do not know whether he *is* a national poet; I know he did not wish to be one. The secret of that paradox is found in his language: an inimitable creation, a rare fusion of everyday speech and the unexpected image. Through that language he discovered that everyday life is enigmatic.

In López Velarde's work, prose and verse form a system of communicating vessels. Villaurrutia wrote that the poet "is almost always present in what we can, without hyperbole, call the *stanzas* of *El minutero*." Phillips completes this observation—which enables us to read the texts in prose more easily—with another that assists us in understanding the poems more completely. In his prose, López Velarde gives us certain keys to his aesthetic, though never in the form of statements. Its unity is organic, not intellectual. A simultaneous reading of his prose and his verse permits us to test the lucidity of his ideas about the world and language, as well as the authenticity of his poems. The results, as always happens with all true poets, prove the coherence between the creative instinct and the critical conscience. In López Velarde's vision the world gives itself to us as sensation and emotion: "The orange is not positivist or Aristotelian in the lyric; it is, simply, an orange. We know only one thing: the world is magic." To proclaim that the world is magic means that objects and beings *are animated* and that one same energy moves man and things. It is the role of the poet to name that energy, to isolate it, and to concentrate it into a poem. Every poem is a diminutive world of attractions and repulsions, a field of magical relationships, and thus a double of the real world. The force that unites and separates things is called Eros:

> *In my happy breast there was no thing*
> *of crystal, clay, or wood*
> *that in my embrace did not assume*
> *the human movements of a wife.*

Things do not order themselves according to the hierarchies of science, philosophy, or morality. The value of objects does not reside in their utility or in their worldly significance (logical or historical), but rather in their vivacity: what unites them to other objects is a kind of universal copulation that transforms them into things never seen before. The metaphor is the agent of change and its mode of action is the embrace. Everyday things—tub, telephone, candlewick, sugar and its slow dissolving, the creaking complaint of an old armoire—contain a greater charge of magical energy than do those things traditionally named by poets. Colloquial expressions, utensils, and everyday situations suffer a happy metamorphosis. Even trash is subject to redemption, as shown in these lines from "El perro de San Roque" [The dog from San Roque]:

> *My flesh is combustible and my conscience dark;*
> *my passions, ephemeral and sharp, glitter*

like the shards of bottle glass that bristled
on the henyard wall to keep out cats and thieves.

López Velarde does not propose so much to conquer the marvelous—
the creation of another reality—as to discover the true reality of things
and of himself. His design is magical: through the medium of the
metaphor he wants to compel things to turn back upon themselves to
become what they truly are. The world is never fully the world—López
Velarde had a very acute awareness of our deficiency in "being"—except in those few privileged moments it is not too much to call electric.
Those instants are the sensations, the emotions, the illuminations afforded us by certain infrequent experiences. The metaphor must be the
equivalent, that is, the analogical double, of those exceptional states:
hence its concentration, its apparent obscurity, and its paradoxes. But
how can things be themselves if the metaphor—the universal embrace
—changes them into other things? López Velarde does not conceive of
language as clothing reality. Instead, language is vesture that reveals
as it conceals. The function of the metaphor is to denude: "For transcendental acts—sleep, bathing, love—we disrobe." The poetic art is the
science of illumination. Its clarity denudes, and sometimes strips away
the skin. Its light is unbearable: "Its supreme brilliance obliges good
people to stay in the shadows, as if they found Sirius instead of a lamp
at their bedsides. Throughout the ages almost everyone who has asked
for literary clarity has actually been asking for a moderation of light,
in order to protect the retina from shock, within a routine penumbra."
Thus, poetry is bedazzlement as well as revelation.

The province is one of López Velarde's themes. Or, more accurately,
it is a magnetic field toward which he turns time and time again, never
returning completely. He is not moved by its sentiments alone; the
province is one dimension of his aesthetic. Life in the cities and towns
of the interior—"cruel sky and red earth"—offers him a world of situations, beings, and things untouched by the Modernist poets. Certainly,
the Mexican Revolution, despoiling some places, repopulating others,
dispersing and reuniting people, and revealing to all of them an unknown land, contributed to the discovery of the province. In López
Velarde's hands this raw material suffers the same transformation

undergone by objects in everyday use and by everyday language. Subjected to the double pressure of verbal alchemy and irony, country simplicity is converted into a rare condiment, one more oddity encrusted upon the discourse of traditional poetry. The most notable example of this metamorphosis is found in "El retorno maléfico" [The malefic return]. Confronting the prodigal son who has returned to the paternal home, the plaster medallions on the door half-close their "narcotized eyelids," look at each other, and say, "What is this?" In the patio there is "a brooding curbstone of a well, with a leather pail dripping its categorical drop." In the garden there is "the loving love of the paired pairs." The art of contrasts: the eruption of "the policeman blowing his whistle" and the warbling of the old maid singing an aria no longer in style accentuate the somnambulistic character of the evocation. The girls who appear some verses later, "fresh and humble as humble cabbages," could be as simple as one wants (soon we will see they are not so simple), but the image the poet has chosen for exhibiting them, "by the light of dramatic streetlights," is one of devilish simplicity.

"Humildemente" [Humbly] offers a series of "slides" of village streets at the hour of the Most Holy Sacrament. Beings and things are immobilized, like "mechanical toys that have run down."

> *My cousin, with her needle*
> *poised, behind her window,*
> *immobile, like a statue . . .*
> *Genoveva's damp*
> *brassiere, set out*
> *to dry, no longer dances*
> *above the tile roof . . .*

The viaticum and the brassiere. Not two symbols: two realities. From a picturesque and ironic scene the poem passes to veneration: the oranges "cease to grow," everything is "on its knees, foreheads in the dust . . ." Not with a leap, but with an imperceptible movement, the description becomes song, and the song, silence. This vision of the province is not local-colorist but magical. López Velarde's aesthetic descends from baroque art—need one recall the Góngora of "Hermana

Marica" [Little sister María]?—and tends toward a very Spanish kind of expressionism. (López Velarde would correct me, saying "and Latin American.") His nationalism springs from his aesthetic—not the reverse. It is a part of his love of the reality that we observe unattentively every day, reality awaiting eyes that will recover it. López Velarde's nationalism is a *discovery*, while that of his imitators is a complacent repetition of what has already been said. In a much-quoted article he speaks of the "newness of the fatherland." A common or ordinary nationalist would have written "the ancientness (or the eternity or the greatness) of the fatherland." What he calls "criollismo" ("native to the New World") is an aesthetic attitude: we should use the words we all say because they are new words, words *never said* in poetry.

Furthermore, the province has spiritual significance. If one thinks in spatial terms, it is what is distant and closed. If one passes from the physical to the moral, it is what is intact and untouchable: feminine virginity, masculine wholeness. Its town, mutilated by the grapeshot of civil war, is a "subverted Eden," a razed paradise to which "it would be better not to return." But the war and the dispersion that have disfigured the town have also made an exile and a cripple of López Velarde. On his spirit, and on his body, too, are the "melancholy maps": the wounds of loves, doubts, angers, resignations, all the acts and omissions of an unsheltered consciousness. He knows the cities; he is the prodigal who enters the house of his infancy on "newcomer's feet" to find that nobody recognizes him. A child's paradise or a reign of adolescent passion, the province is not so much a point in space as it is nostalgia for unrecoverable well-being. López Velarde knows that, and as a defense he uses irony: through the alleyways of Zacatecas—so uneven in footing they are a "bad joke"—file "Catholics from the age of Peter the Hermit and Jacobins from the Tertiary Age." And, nevertheless, the enchantment persists. His natal town "tempts with an alluring combination of fossil and miniature." He sees himself wandering through the streets: "I am nothing more than an abandoned beast passing through a fictitious town. Once I am in bed, lying as if in a sarcophagus, the clock in the sanctuary sounds twelve. Thunder rolls, and everything becomes futile." A bitter vision: has the province died or is it López Velarde who is dead? A symbol of physical distance and lost innocence, the province belongs to the *before* and the *after*. It is a temporal dimension: it embodies the past, but at the same time it prefigures what will again be. That future is identified with death: Eden will open only to the dying. The relationship between López Velarde and the province is the same as that joining him with Fuensanta, his symbol of spiritual woman. Both represent distance that only death can abolish:

> *When, at the end, exhaustion*
> *overcomes me,*
> *I shall go, like the crane*
> *in the proverb, to my town . . .*

It is difficult to talk about *La suave patria* [Gentle fatherland]. This beautiful and luckless poem does not deserve to have been treated so badly. (Or is its fate at the hands of the public the sort experienced by all provocative and too-evident beauty?) I shall begin by saying that *La suave patria* tolerates sentimental but not ideological complicities. Whatever his political opinions may have been, and they were never very ardent, López Velarde did not confuse art with preachment or the poem with the harangue. He had a natural aversion to systems and preferred beings and things to ideas: "The fatherland is not a historical or political reality but an intimate one." With this declaration, contemporary with the publication of the poem, López Velarde, without proposing to do so, places himself at the opposite pole from the Mexican mural painting that was beginning in precisely those years. So, for semantic convenience or out of adherence to historical classifications, he can be called a poet of the Revolution—but never a revolutionary poet. His attitude, furthermore, has been almost constantly that of all modern Mexican poetry. Although today the pressures, insults, and flattery have ceased—our own dangers are different—it is good to recall this tradition of moral integrity.

La suave patria is not a poem concerned with national glories or disasters. As he begins, López Velarde informs us: "I shall navigate through civil waves with weightless oars . . ." And he fulfills that notice: there are scarcely any allusions to the political or social history of Mexico or to its heroes, political bosses, tyrants, or saviors. The only historical episode he considers worthy of separate mention intrigues him by its legendary nature. The ten lines that evoke Cuauhtémoc's crossing the lake in his pirogue to give himself up to Cortés contain memorable images: the "sobbing of mythologies"; the king who tears himself away from the "curved bosom" of the queen "as from the breast of a partridge"; and those "swimming idols" in which I see the whole catastrophe—water and fire—of Tenochtitlán. The remainder of the poem is a portrait of the countryside and of life during that epoch in Mexico. Realism? Yes, on the condition that one call realistic our anonymous nineteenth-century painters and those who, since Le Douanier Rousseau, have been rather inappropriately called "modern primitives." The poem is a succession of colors, tastes, perfumes, and sensations; it is not a fresco but a documentary, in the cinematic sense, of poetic images.

The real equivalent to *La suave patria* can be found in the theater rather than in painting or film. Neither lyric nor heroic—its tone is the "muted epic"—it is a drama/poem divided into two acts, with an introduction and an entr'acte. The introduction functions like the prologue of a romantic comedy or like an orchestral overture at the opera: it serves as a declaration of the author's intentions, not discounting self-irony, and as the entrance of the instruments, with a predominance of strings and percussion. The entr'acte is a solo in which the vocalist, occasionally accompanied by a distant murmur of flageolets, recites the torture of a hero. The two acts, performed by the whole company, are composed of a series of theater scenes: there is no dialogue. Dialogue is supplanted, to the poem's advantage, by pantomime and dance. There is no action: the ending of a fiesta, the appearance of the "allegorical straw cart," the rustic throne of Pomona-Guadalupe-Tonantzín. A spectacle for the eye and the ear, *La suave patria* more closely resembles the music of Silvestre Revueltas than mural painting. In its genre, the poem is perfect. There are fragments one will not easily forget: the thunder of the tempest that maddens our women and "cures the lunatic"; a mestizo girl's gaze that places "immensity over their hearts"; "opaque Lent"; "birds of the carpentry profession" [woodpeckers]; and many others. No one but López Velarde could have written those lines. The poem is, in a certain way, the noonday of his style. I am saying the noonday of his style, not of his poetry. Mastery frequently defeats inspiration, formula substitutes for invention, mere cleverness supplants the true discovery. The poet's gaze does not penetrate either his own reality or that of his people. It is an external poem.

López Velarde is a difficult poet and he proclaims a difficult aesthetic. His hatred for the "coarse speech of the masses" is the obverse of his love for the expression that dazzles us with its rightness. Thus, it is the genuine he seeks, more than the surprising. His originality lies in his penetrating toward origins, toward what is most ancient: in his search for roots. To him a poem is not a recently manufactured object, it is a recently unearthed talisman. Novelty and surprise are the two wings of a poem, and without them there is no poetry; but the body of a poem is the discovery of a timeless reality. For López Velarde, expression is synonymous with exploration of self, and both are synonymous with self-creation. He does not wish to say what he feels; he wishes to discover who he is and what he feels in order to feel it more fully, to be what he is with greater freedom. That quest for himself leads to the quest for the "other reality," because man is never entirely himself; always unfinished, he completes himself only when he goes outside himself and invents himself. López Velarde's artistic passion has a spiritual meaning. His critical conscience is not merely aesthetic. Or perhaps it is so rigorously aesthetic that it blends with life itself. He polishes—not as an artificer, but as a lover—each noun and each verb infinitely, because in each one of them he gambles with his identity. To lose the game is to forget oneself, not know oneself, lose something more than glory or fame: life's reason for being. In the spiritual history of our poetry, López Velarde is the scrupulous balance. He cares about adjectives because he cares about his soul.

2 . THE PURPLE STAIN

In his breast a magnet
shaped like a clover
and of the passionate hue of a poppy . . .
　　　　　　Ramón López Velarde

Love is his theme. In this, too, he is exceptional, because, in spite of what is generally believed, this passion is not present in modern Mexican poetry to the same extent that it is in the work of López Velarde.[4] The two moments into which his work is divided, *La sangre devota* and *Zozobra*, are ruled by two different woman figures. His amorous experience is so closely bound to his verbal adventure that for the majority of his critics Fuensanta, the love of his youth, and the unidentified women of *Zozobra* and *El son del corazón* symbolize two styles of versification as well as two kinds of love. This opinion, although essentially accurate, is too divisive. *La sangre devota* is not an entirely ingenuous book (the ambiguity of the title suggests that), nor is Fuensanta a metaphysical shade. Other disquieting figures appear in addition to Fuensanta, such as that cousin Agueda—green eyes and ceremonious mourning—who is contemplated by the poet with the fixed and at the same time giddy gaze of adolescent desire. On the other hand, I am not sure whether the word "love" correctly expresses the contradictory sentiments that Fuensanta inspired in him. Perhaps, at the beginning, López Velarde was not actually aware of that complexity, but it is certain that later he fully realized the singular nature of their relationship. In a poem inspired by that first love he says: "You give me . . . something that is a mixture of cordial consolation and the glacial forlornness of a maiden's bed." The opposition between "cordial" and

---

4. In Salvador Díaz Mirón there is erotic sculpture, not love; in Manuel José Othón, praise of the isolated life (the exception: the half-dozen sonnets that comprise "Idilio salvaje" [Savage idyll], almost the only thing still alive among his vast production); Enrique González Martínez, or meditation; Juan José Tablada, or the voyage; and so on. Among the *contemporáneos*: Xavier Villaurrutia, or the dialogue between the insomniac and the somnambulist; José Gorostiza, or the monologue of water in its tomb of transparencies; Carlos Pellicer, or poetic flight; Gilberto Owen, or the angel in the subway; and so on. Another exception: *Nuevo amor* [New love], Salvador Novo's beautiful book. Naturally, I am not saying that love does not exist in these poets' works. Without love there is no poetry. What I am saying is that for them it was not the tyrannical preoccupation that it was for López Velarde.

"glacial" hinders the consummation of that love, and at the same time that mixture keeps it alive through the years. Since that love formed of contradictory elements is a *confusion*, the consolation and the forlornness, the glacial and the cordial, do not blend together, but neither are they separate. The ambiguity does not reside only in the object of López Velarde's adoration but also in his emotions: to love Fuensanta as a woman is to betray the devotion he professes for her; to venerate her as a spirit is to forget that she is also, and first of all, flesh and blood. So that this love may endure, the confusion must be preserved, but at the same time its contradictions must be avoided. His love is constant fluctuation between the two poles that define it. Thus he cannot expose his love to the proof of reality without exposing it to extinction: blood and devotion will finally blend together, or one will annihilate the other. The only recourse is to transform it. Fuensanta becomes an inaccessible body and his love for her something that will never be embodied in the here and now. He is not confronted by an impossible love; his love is impossible because its essence is a permanent but never consummated possibility.

López Velarde was too lucid not to know that by evading the alternatives, consummation or disillusion, he was sacrificing the real Fuensanta and the reality of her love. His attitude condemns his beloved to a kind of perpetual limbo, wandering between the before and the after. She is what could have been, so she appears always as a remote creature, in other time and other space. She embodies the provinces and the ingenuous, but not innocent, pleasures of adolescence: she is what *was*, and she will again *be* in "apocalyptic time," in the afterworld. Fuensanta, a real woman, becomes a shadow. While the other women of his poems are an immediate presence, whether fierce or merry, Fuensanta is the image of distance. She is the lost, the soul in pain, the absent one with whom one maintains an imaginary dialogue. She is that which is about to leave us and which for an instant we still retain: you are, he says to her, "an epistle written in moribund strokes of the pen, replete with dramatic adieus." Although not the best of López Velarde, these lines express very well what that love was: an interminable farewell.

Distance is not enough. Even when distant, Fuensanta's reality is a menace to his devotion. Death is the most perfect form of farewell.

Dead, Fuensanta will be more fully "what could have been" and, since both believed in resurrection, "what must one day be." Anticipating the reality, López Velarde imagines her death agony. There are two revealing texts: one a poem, one written in prose. As surprising as the fact that in both López Velarde presents himself as the angel of death is the cruel precision of the invented details. In the poem, Fuensanta will see, "in the mirror of her armoire," the writing of a skeletal hand, and she "will cry out the five letters of [the poet's] name"; but he "will not be present at the final anguish." Is this a vision of pain or of revenge? Perhaps both. It is a sacrifice in which one of the two participants, and not precisely the victim, is a phantom. In the second instance, López Velarde repeats the scene with greater realism: "The shadow of your death agony will darken beneath your eyes, and you will think of me and find it more difficult to breathe . . ." In the poem López Velarde's absence made the dying girl's final agony more total; in the prose fragment his absence contributes physically to her death: it suffocates her, asphyxiates her. Something more than fear of losing the beloved leads him to imagine this atrocious death. It is an invoked, a desired death. There will be someone, of course, who says that this is the typical extravagant expression of all lovers. Others will say that destroying what we most love, even in dreams, is one of the strangest and most powerful components of passion. But it would be wiser to ask oneself whether López Velarde truly loved Fuensanta. I think that, more than love, he experienced that combination of emotions that he calls devotion. Passion would have led him to profane his devotion; the eroticism of his imagination, not without its aggressiveness, moves him to sacrifice symbolically the object he venerates.

Hope for a new meeting throbs implicitly in every farewell. No one, saying good-by, dares to say that it is forever. Fuensanta's death, the real and the imaginary, has a paradoxical consequence: it has become a symbol more of encounter than of farewell. In an intense poem he never finished, "El sueño de los guantes negros" [The dream of the black gloves], López Velarde tells of the lovers' reunion. In the first line he tells us the poem is a dream. Its hallucinatory clarity, its pure colors and strict design, the preciseness of that end-of-the-world landscape and the sensations that overwhelm us as we delve into those strophes of concentric resonances, the apparition of the two phantasmal figures in the center of the great salt basin, and, finally, even the two or three blank lines—all this makes the poem a true vision in the religious sense of the word: a waking dream. As with many of his poems—the first to notice it was Tablada, who called the elegy he dedicated to López Velarde's memory an "altarpiece"—this composition is a painting, a small canvas. It reminds me of the fantastical realism of some of the Flemish painters. The strangeness of the world López Velarde paints does not reside in its forms but in the atmosphere in which they are bathed. It is the everyday world—seen beneath a new light. The same is true of the female apparition: nothing denotes her extraterrestrial condition except the fact that she appears wearing "black gloves." Those funereal gloves recall the luxurious hats of Cranach's nudes. The poet asks himself: "Does your flesh still cling to every bone?" He himself does not know:

> *The enigma of love was entirely veiled*
> *beneath the prudence of your black gloves . . .*

Reunited finally, their hands clasped as if they held together the "edifice of the universe," the lovers whirled in "an eternal circuit." The separation has ended, but true union is impossible, as is suggested by the prudence of the black gloves. The poem seems to be less the consecration of a consummated love than the presentiment of an eternal damnation. And the reader is tempted to ask Nerval's question: "Is she dead or is she Death?"

All of López Velarde's erotic life occurred between the time of Fuensanta's symbolic death and the time of her imaginary resurrection. All his life, and all his work, too, since he wrote his two principal books during those years (*Zozobra* and *El minutero*). It would not be accurate to say that this period broke with the preceding one. In reality it prolonged it, it exacerbated it, and it made it more lucid (always considering that one already foresees the tone of his mature poetry in several poems from *La sangre devota*; for example, "A Sara" [To Sara]). His new loves, including his second great passion, more sensual but no less complex than the first, are the cruel continuation of the experience of his youth. Distance and death render Fuensanta inaccessible; proximity and death make the others so. The embrace is a metaphor for the skeleton and the skull. The glacial and the cordial are now definitively one. That mystery fascinates him to such a degree that it accompanies him everywhere; it is inseparable from his vision of the world and of life. One might say that it is the mystery tattooed on the body of woman: the organs of gestation are those of our destruction. If the male is the extravagance and self-indulgence of the species, the female is its continuity: she perpetuates herself by devouring us. Although the idea is not new, it is more than a commonplace to López Velarde: it is a revelation that guides him in his exploration of reality and of himself. Through it he penetrates certain forbidden zones. There, in vaster and more inclement spaces, truth opens like a cruel double flower.

Woman is the most complete and perfect image of the universe because in her are united the two halves of being; she is also the sensitive mirror in which for an instant man may see himself in all his dolorous unreality. But woman is something more than a world image and something more than a mirror for man. She also shares our universal lack of "being," a deprivation that expresses itself as a rabid, destructive hunger for death. The vision of a reclining body as a landscape of signs wherein we read the obverse and reverse of reality is replaced by another, active vision that invites us not to contemplation but to the embrace. That embrace, the poet emphasizes many times, is bloody: it is "the purple stain." Does the monologue cease, the solitary conversation with the always absent one? López Velarde never found a partner for his dialogue, except perhaps at some instant in his second passion; on the other hand, he knew amorous adversaries. The feminine body is no longer fruit, a guitar to be caressed or wounded; it acquires will and soul and stands opposing the male. Eroticism does not reveal woman to him, it reveals her terrible freedom—something very different from feminine emancipation, a theme that most certainly would not have interested him. When he discovers in woman that active element he thought to be man's privilege and condemnation, the word "pleasure" and the abysmal reality it designates, those qualities immediately change in coloration and meaning.

In woman's erotic freedom he recognizes his own, and on these two hostile freedoms he founds a brotherhood. It is a vertiginous fraternity because it is founded on the instant: a foundation resting on an abyss. A secret society in which neither name nor rank nor morality matter, it shelters alike the girl whose name he cannot recall, Sara, that "cluster of ripe grapes," the married woman, and the "woman without either cunning or disguises." This is not a society of libertines, but solitary beings united in private rituals. Provincial virgins are also part of that clandestine fraternity. They are symbols of rebellion and submission and thus doubly his sisters, and he watches them come out on their balconies in the early evenings

> *so that their sexual parts may drink the breeze*
> *like maddened scorpions.*

Once again López Velarde surprises us with an image that is a cruel and precise sketch. Reading these lines, one is forcibly reminded of Julio Ruelas, that small great artist still awaiting recognition from our critics. It is a drypoint whose lines turn back upon themselves in order to concentrate all the more the blood's exasperation: there is no pity in that clear view of woman, rather something that might be called complicity. Sisters or accomplices, López Velarde is united to them by a bond stronger than blood or baptism. In the solitude of a room closed to the external world, an urban cavern or the "lost bedchamber of the necromancer," they have shared with him a few hours outside chronological time: lust, weariness, the savor of crime and of innocence, abandon, and concentration. Together they have crossed, eyes closed, that "bridge across abysses" that love extends from one body to another.

Imagination is active desire. We desire the forms we imagine, but those images adopt the form our desire has imposed upon them. Finally, we return to ourselves: we have pursued our own shadow, without ever touching it. Eroticism is a discharge of imagination and thus has no limits except those our nature defines (that is, each person's power of invention and his psychical conformation as much as, or more than, his body). Or to say it another way: eroticism is infinitude at the service of our finitude. Thus its combinations, practically uncountable, finally seem monotonous to us. They are: their diversity is repetition. The libertine proposes the abolition of the other and so converts that person into an "erotic object." Each body he touches evaporates into smoke, and each of his experiences is annulled as it is fulfilled. His action is a pilgrimage toward an always imminent point that perpetually fades, reappears, and again disappears. The solitary imagination is circular, boredom as well as disenchantment await us at the end of each circuit. One may be vicious because of weakness, foolishness, lack of imagination, or any other defect of body or soul. One is a libertine only by reason of asceticism, as is revealed in *The Story of O* and other guides of initiation, or because of philosophical conviction, as is abundantly illustrated by the Marquis de Sade. In each and every case the reward is not pleasure, knowledge, or power but *insensibility*. A state of indifference already described by the ancient Stoics and by the philosophers of India, except that the road of libertinism is longer and more painful and its results are more uncertain. Love, on the other hand, is born not of the imagination but of vision. The lover does not invent, he recognizes. His imagination is not free: he must confront this mystery, the loved one. The lover is condemned to guessing, although he knows beforehand that both the question and the answer are illusory, what is going on behind that brow and what attracts those eyes: "What are you thinking, at whom are you looking?" Happy or unhappy, satisfied or disdained, he who loves must reckon with the other; her presence imposes a limitation upon the lover and thus leads him to the recognition of his finitude. This limitation opens another realm, this one truly unlimited, to his imagination. Eroticism is an infinite multiplication of finite bodies; love is the discovery of infinitude in one single being.

López Velarde sought love all his life. It does not matter whether he found it or whether, as is more probable, he did not wish to find it because he was more enamored of love itself than of any woman. In a poem from his earliest writing he confesses that he suffers from an "infinite thirst for love." He does not say his love is infinite: he says his thirst is. His work lives on that fragile frontier separating eroticism from love, and in this, perhaps, resides the secret of its seduction. His beloved ones are his sisters because with them he has shared the mystery. He recognizes himself in them and they in him. This fraternity is a constant presence in his spirit and, like obsessions, it assumes two forms: the harem and the hospital. The time that binds him to all those women is that of their common destiny: "runaway time." Although he would have wished to arrest their "dark fall" with his own hands, he can only watch as they hurl themselves into the abyss. Their fall is his fall. To López Velarde the metaphor of passion, the embrace, means that *together* they hurl themselves from the precipice. Woman reveals to him the true face of death as she shows him, with such abandon, the true face of life—but, as she embraces his body, she too glimpses the truth that what she clasps to her bosom is a heap of bones. Even though its root is erotic this experience goes beyond eroticism. Nor is it love. I would not call it passion, but compassion.

It has been stated too often that López Velarde is "the poet of eroticism and death." This formula is too vague. If his love is funereal and if in every body he embraces a skeleton, the opposite is also true. Death is erotic. Facing death he feels the same excitement he feels before a woman. Although he fears it, he cannot take his eyes from it. To contend that he is in love with death would be foolish, as well as excessive. Also, in a certain sense, we are all in love with death, aware of the same unconscious attraction we feel toward the mother and the earth. Death is one of man's centers of gravity. But that is not the case here. López Velarde's feeling is more violent and more contradictory. Death terrifies him, but he cannot reduce the sensation he is experiencing either to terror or to subconscious attraction. His mouth "is placed upon the skeleton's femininity with a diamond cutter's scrupulous care." These expressions are not part of the vocabulary of fear or of adoration, but of pleasure. Death seems desirable to him and there is a moment when he confuses it with the vertigo of passion:

> *My kisses travel across you in devout files*
> *above a sacrilegious stratum of skulls*
> *as if over an erotic domino.*

Kisses, devotion, sacrilege, skulls: this enumeration, evoking a kind of cheap symbolism, is suddenly redeemed in that disconcerting and marvelous last line. In another poem, "La última odalisca," López Velarde reveals what that fascination consists of: on the waist of "voluptuous melancholy"—always that union of oppositions—pleasure writes its "calligraphy" and death its "scrawl." Pleasure and death are two faces of the same coin. This idea, also, is not original, but the intensity with which he lives it and the forms it adopts in his poetry and his life *are* original. Death terrifies him as the end or extinction of man; and, simultaneously, it seduces him because *it is the abysmal element of the embrace.* In many poems he reiterates his terror of the inevitable putrefaction of the body; at the same time he asserts that the presence of death in the midst of the embrace transforms a more or less instinctual act into a spiritual experience. The intensity of desire makes that instant of union a union beyond the instant; the awareness of death introduces time into this frenzy; that instant is a mortal instant, and, precisely because of that, it separates itself from chronology and becomes an instant that is unique and absolute. Lovers walk above the void. Consciousness of their mortality is the force that launches them beyond time and retains them in time. There is a kind of metaphysical intoxication in that floating upon an instant that rests on nothing except itself, with nothing to grasp except another body equally detached from its name and its moorings. López Velarde says it in a few unforgettable lines:

> . . . *the blessing of love is an unbridled*
> *heart galloping along the cliff road*
> *of death . . .*

At a distance halfway between libertinism and permanent union, López Velarde decided to inhabit the instant. There is no hedonism in his choice. To select the instant is to choose not pleasure, but lucidity. In reality, it is a refusal to choose at all, it is to accept everything. López Velarde's "capacity for feeling shelters beneath the insignia of the lubricous barometer" that reflects all changes, all situations, and all beings:

> . . . *woman, a star,*
> *the anguish of thunder, the staff of old age,*
> *a griffin vomiting his hydraulic complaint,*
> *and a lamp, the blinking eye of the tabernacle.*

López Velarde's attitude is not inspired by desire for domination, will for power, vanity, or cynicism. Perpetually bewildered by "quarrelsome eyes and peaceful brows," he believes in surrender. He is never the seducer, his "soul is a worshiper." No, López Velarde chose love and, *at the same time*, solitude. All his life he was loyal to this contradictory decision. His work is the emblem of his loyalty. And one must add that he thought he had engraved the signs of human existence on that emblem.

His love, as he knew better than we, was not total love. Knew? At least he guessed. Phillips cites various poems, dedicated to the woman who was his second love, in which he reiterates that he is indebted to her for revealing "life's perfect savor." Perhaps for a while love was no longer that mixture of the glacial and the cordial or that anguish of feeling himself "hanging in the ceaseless agility of the ether," represented, respectively, by Fuensanta and his passing love affairs. His poetry, a true barometer of the alterations in his sensitivity, changed radically. This was the highest point of his amorous fever and also the moment of the greatest concentration of his creative gifts. He wrote his best poems in those months: on the one hand, through Lugones he had discovered his own style; on the other, his new love revealed to him the true temper of his soul. His eroticism is exacerbated and flows more deeply, turned upon itself like water working upon a stone the signs of its destruction. Intoxication and lucidity. Fuensanta had been a passive figure, more idol than reality; the second woman is simultaneously body and spirit: an untouchable body that bewitches him, a spirit that frightens him and opens unknown worlds to him. She is a "pale vehemence," and in order to accentuate even more the contradiction of that figure he adds: "Did you do penance wallowing in the wilderness?" For the first and last time López Velarde recognizes in a woman a spiritual complexity similar to his own. For an instant, woman is no longer an object of veneration or pleasure: "The conflagration has touched your face, and lava has flowed over it." He owes to her the revelation of his "own zodiac: the Lion and the Virgin." The discovery of himself is also that of one woman who is all women, "total and partial, peripheral and central"; that is, a woman who is able to be a lover without abdicating her own will. Freedom. In spite of the exasperated sensuality of his expressions, always oscillating between the cruelty and the vision of death, his passion is spiritual—if one understands by that a love that does not deny the body but rather scourges and consumes it. The road of his passion is a "ruby road" sprinkled with his own blood. Possession is impossible; but, even if it were not, it would be no different: what is there besides the body? Something, perhaps, that is neither life nor death. All love, even though it be for a fraction of a second, is contemplation of the abyss:

> *Did you lie sleeping on the slope*
> *of a volcano? Did lava pour across your lips*
> *and calcine your brow?*

López Velarde's second love revealed to him the soul's dialogue and the body's monologue—not plenitude. That woman, the one who loved him with a more active, complex, and lucid love than Fuensanta (but did Fuensanta ever love him, ever glimpse the real man?), that woman who was his true mate, the one to whom he owed the discovery of his most secret self, rejected him. Whatever the external reasons for her refusal, by acting in this way she was faithful, perhaps without knowing it, to the temper of their mutual passion. A combustible passion, not an embodied one. We have lost the ancient secret of reconciliation, and our loves humiliate the body or degrade the spirit. Plenitude, for López Velarde, would from that time be "beyond": either poetry or death. With bitterness, but without rancor, he settled definitively into his solitude. Again he became "the cosmic beggar." It will be said by some that he did not choose to be a bachelor, but that it was imposed on him by circumstances, as it had been, similarly, by Fuensanta. I do not agree. I need scarcely dwell on our individual responsibility in what we call our failures, whether it be in love or in other areas of life. Unconscious or unconfessed, that responsibility is still ours. Do we not almost always seek what harms us; are we not the secret authors of our ruin? If man is not the master of his destiny, neither is he entirely its victim. We are accomplices of our circumstances: López Velarde *knew* beforehand that their love was unrealizable, although he would never have admitted it to himself. Furthermore, two facts prove that his choice was voluntary: throughout his life he professed an aversion to matrimony and, what is more momentous and more definitive, he never hid his repugnance of fatherhood.

Perhaps scandalized by the frankness of his statements, the majority of his critics have not paused long enough to examine López Velarde's ideas on procreation, or they have preferred to hide them behind a curtain of sentimental explanations. Nevertheless, the poet could not have been more explicit: the family is "a factory of suffering, a source of disgrace, a seed bed of misfortune." In the same text—a short story with an autobiographical flavor—he compares the family hearth to a beast's den and the cries and laughter of the young to the moans and curses of the damned: ". . . in the somber and asphyxiating hub of fecundity, where Rosario, like all the other women, would multiply the groans and blasphemies of the stock of Cain." The violence of this language could lead us to believe that we are dealing with a momentary catharsis. But no: we are confronting something more profound: López Velarde made a vow not to have children—and he fulfilled it. His decision was meditated, and, in spite of what critics think, it is not in contradiction to the other aspects of his character. (He was a complex, not a contradictory, spirit.) Without fear or reticence, the devotee of the roundabout, of the oblique allusion, confides his thoughts to us: "It is more worthy to lead a sterile life than to prolong the corruption beyond ourselves. . . . Why populate the cemetery? I shall live this hour of melody, of calm and light, for myself and my offspring. Thus I shall live it with an incisive intensity, the intensity of one who wishes in his lifetime to live the life of his race." His misanthropy is not, at least not exclusively, the result of his character or his misfortunes, but of his reflections. He loves life; he affirms that he will enjoy the hour that has been given him with lucid fullness because he knows it will be his last. All this, which is a great deal, seems nothing to him. In the same paragraph in which he exalts life—light, melody, calm—he condemns it. And he goes further: life seems admirable to him because it will not be repeated: the hour is beautiful because it is the last. His condemnation is definitive. In fact, he exalts death. And he exalts it as an absolute reality: only death liberates us from corruption, only death can give us the sensation of totality that time perpetually denies us. In the light of this confidence the image of life as a harem and a hospital finally appears in all its gravity. It is something more than a psychological anomaly, something different from the fantasy of a flayed sensitivity: it is a *judgment* about the world and about the value of existence. Life suffers from an invisible and incurable infection. Although we call that illness Time, its true name is Evil. To propagate life is to serve the devil.

3. THE SOUND OF THE HEART

Soul, inseparable sibyl, I no longer know where you end and where I begin; we are two turns of the same refulgent knot, of the same knot of love.

Ramón López Velarde

We lack a truly complete study of López Velarde's beliefs. I say beliefs, not ideas, because except in exceptional cases, like that of his denial of the value of existence, his convictions were more felt than thought. As he frequently observed, his Catholicism was not without its doubts and vacillations. He never lived out those doubts as a drama of the intellect. In moments of crisis he resorted to the power of grace, not to the consolation of theology. He founds his orthodoxy on the purity of his feelings; his sins are sins of love and only love can pardon them. His childhood religion forms his vital base; it is nourishment for his spiritual life: its rites are a kind of superior aesthetic, a ceremonial for souls; its mysteries are a theater without time whose symbols represent the passion of truth. But López Velarde is his own audience; his fervor seems to him lightly comic, and he treats his beliefs with a certain ironic tenderness. He does not believe, but he cannot stop believing. He scorns the fanatics of the new cult, the "measly journalists" who clutch in their fists "the torch of progress" and rail against the "hydra of obscurantism." He asserts: "My heart is retrograde." The adjective is double-edged: he is Catholic to the rationalists, idolater to the Christians. It does not embarrass him to confess that he is superstitious—and as he makes his confession a skeptical smile touches his lips.

Ever since Villaurrutia used it to define López Velarde's poetry, all possible meanings have been wrung from the following celebrated sentence: "The synthesis of my zodiac is the Lion and the Virgin." It is amazing that no one has remarked on the first and most obvious meaning of this declaration. Instead of rushing to psychology manuals, commentators might have leafed through any astrology tract. Phillips touches on this theme, commenting that astronomical motifs are frequent in López Velarde's poetry and prose, "especially those of the signs of the zodiac." It would have been more accurate to say *astrological* motifs. It cannot be denied that López Velarde was interested in the occult sciences, an inclination shared with several modern poets. It is his second love, teaching him to breathe in this atmosphere of exalted spiritualism mixed with apocalyptic visions—as we glimpse in *El don de febrero*—to whom he owes this vision of his being ruled by the dual and contradictory influences of the sun and Mercury. Symbols of the cabala, astrology, and alchemy also appear in his poems. One of the most perfect compositions, from a certain point of view perhaps the most accomplished, in *Zozobra* is titled "Día trece" [The thirteenth day] and ends with an invocation to the dark powers: "Superstition: help me hold the radiant vertigo of the everlasting moment . . ." He does not see superstition as an error on the part of the ancients but rather as the remnants of a lost wisdom not entirely incompatible with modern beliefs: "I respect equally the physicist who sees in his shadow the propagation of light . . . and the savage who venerates his own shadow. Astrology, when it pleases her, enters my bed with her chilly feet. I depend on chiromancy as I do on vaccine. I confuse the laws of Newton with those of fate. My cabala credo. My amulet art." All this is difficult to reconcile with Catholic dogma, but it does not harm what I would call López Velarde's emotional orthodoxy. His pessimism is a more serious matter.

To deny oneself procreation because existence is evil is a heresy the church has never pardoned. I do not know what readings inspired this idea in him. Although identification of sources is very important, it is not indispensable. I will simply mention that at that time certain Oriental concepts were beginning to be known among us. In those years Tablada was interested in Buddhism and Vasconcelos in Indian philosophy. Critics consider "La última odalisca" to be one of the central poems of *Zozobra* and judge it, and rightly so, to be a true key to his poetry. Even so, as far as I am aware no one has remarked on the Oriental flavor of its first two stanzas. The first follows:

> *My flesh is heavy and resigned*
> *because its fabulous weight*
> *is the shuddering chain*
> *of the universal bodies*
> *that have united themselves with my life.*

One scarcely need comment on these five lines: pantheism and, not entirely explicit, reincarnation and karma. It would not be difficult to find other scattered examples. But López Velarde's contact with Oriental thought must not have been either very intimate or very prolonged. He did not need to go so far afield to identify procreation with evil. He received this idea from a more direct, though never wholly visible, tradition that has been a secret and perpetual current circulating throughout the history of the West.

However indifferent he may have been to theology, it is impossible to believe that López Velarde was unaware that his condemnation of existence coincided with an ancient heresy combated by the church from the time of its origin, one that still possesses us today, although we at times do not know it: Manichaeism.[5] Do not adduce against this a lack of reading: if we forget that he studied in a seminary we forget a great deal. Neither is it probable, no matter how insecure his knowledge of history, that he did not know about the extermination of the Albigenses at the beginning of the thirteenth century. The Middle Ages interested López Velarde. Alongside allusions to the Scriptures, sacred history, and ecclesiastical liturgy in his work, we find saints, emperors, virgins, crusades, and medieval legends. No less significant is the utilization in his poems of certain symbols from Provençal poetry and the early Renaissance. The enumeration of all these elements would be tiresome. Furthermore, what concerns us is not his erudition or his information but the direction of his poetry.

5. Luis Noyola Vázquez alludes to this theme in *Fuentes de Fuensanta* (Mexico City, 1947).

The duality of matter and spirit, body and soul, sensual and spiritual love can be Christian if the opposition is not definitive; by that I mean, if the two principles are not irreconcilable. The church does not condemn the flesh, rather the confusion that causes us to attribute to the body the virtues of the spirit: the deification of a mortal creature. It judges deviations of the spirit with the same severity, and this explains the mistrust, not to mention hostility, with which it regards mystics. In every lover and in every mystic lies the seed of heresy. But nature is not evil: it is the fallen world. The earth and all living things share with man banishment from "being," contingency. This separation is infinite (the abyss between God and man being insurmountable), not eternal: although redemption will not make us gods, it does extend a bridge between fallen beings and a full state of being. On the other hand, for López Velarde the two halves never become one. The spirit is invulnerable, incorruptible, untouchable. Matter, subject to time, borne down by its own weight, falls; matter is vulnerable and its weight is affliction and corruption. López Velarde's dualism is radical, and it is there that we must find the basis of his pessimism. His prose and poetry contain innumerable allusions to this central theme, which at times becomes an obsession. In "La última odalisca," as a prime example, bodies are "shipwrecked clusters of fruit riding the crest of the Flood," and their weight is "fabulous" because it accumulates all the weightiness of matter and time throughout the centuries. Time is not only multiplicity but also continuity, the proliferation of evil. For that reason the soul, in the following stanza, also is "heavy and afflicted"; its weight is its sorrow, and it consists of having known—being of spiritual essence— "the red grove and the surgeon's knife": love that is time and death. That knowledge is an "arcane distress."

The soul is not the spirit: it is one of its sparks fallen into matter, lost in the labyrinths of time. The soul's salvation cannot consist of the redemption of the natural world postulated by Christianity, but rather of the definitive separation of matter and spirit. Or to put it another way: the annihilation of the body is the condition for the soul's return to its origin. Thus death is a dual potentiality. It is illness, decomposition, extinction, and rebirth: the succession of instants and centuries, the agony of the "cruel logarithmic rush"; but it is also liberation of the soul, the fire that purifies, the breath that annuls the body. Material death is a plurality and pullulation of forms, some atrocious and others enchanting; its essence is to have no essence: it is multiplicity. The death that liberates is unity and has only one form: it is the angel, the beloved, the wife beyond the tomb, Fuensanta. It is Death. The horror of death and the fascination with death that seemed to us to be an aberration and a contradiction are no longer obsessions: they have meaning, they form the axis of a spiritual vision considerably more coherent than the poor disconnected explanations of the psychology of our time. López Velarde is afraid of dying because, like Quevedo, "the world has bewitched" him; and he loves death because he is in love with an incorruptible being, that spirit of which the soul is a fragment. Only love of the death that is Death will save him from the corruption of mortal life.

The resurrection of the flesh signifies, among other things, the redemption of the body. López Velarde passionately believed in that dogma. It will be said that it is impossible to reconcile this belief with the idea that existence is evil. True. But I shall simply repeat that López Velarde did not concern himself with imposing an intellectual system on his work and that I am not looking for such severe order. My intention is different: to discover the relationships and the meaning of his poetic experiment. So, then, did he believe in the resurrection of the flesh, or did he believe he believed? Perhaps "El sueño de los guantes negros," the poem about resurrection, could respond to this question. The nucleus of that composition, its principal line, is not a response but an interrogation: "Does your flesh still cling to every bone?" López Velarde asks himself the same question we ask. And he cannot answer: "The enigma of love was entirely veiled . . ." The response is an indecipherable mystery. One will not perceive the meaning of that terrible doubt unless one knows what and who Fuensanta was in the mythology of the poet.

In an insignificant but revealing poem from his youth, "El adiós" [The farewell], López Velarde calls himself "the idolater": and she is his idol, "the white, light woman." Fuensanta rejects this deification and states that "the cadaver of her love" from that day forward "will preside over his hearth's mourning." Thus, at the moment that she is moving away from him in reality, Fuensanta is joining him in the afterworld. In another composition from those years, even less felicitous ("El campanero" [The bell ringer]), the poet declares that his betrothed is Death. This is a commonplace, but poetry is made of commonplaces that turn into images and unheard-of realities. In the case of López Velarde the sentimental reality of Fuensanta is transfigured, as time passes, into a metaphysical reality. The transformation is ascendant and progresses from the provincial sweetheart to impossible love and from this love to death, "my blood's harmonious elect." In order for the idolatry of youth to be converted into the religion of maturity it is necessary that she pass through the purgatories of eroticism and death. Only dead, now a pure spirit, can the beloved truly be Fuensanta. The question posed in "El sueño de los guantes negros" has an ambiguous resonance. Is Fuensanta not yet a spirit because the poet is still bewitched by time and its pitfalls? What is the significance of those black gloves, whose prudence accentuates even more their funereal eroticism? They are an obstacle, a prohibition, but what do they prohibit? The union of their souls or of their bodies? The lovers whirl in an eternal circuit— an image that recalls a celebrated passage from the *Divine Comedy*— without ever joining together, without ever being either wholly dead or wholly alive, in a landscape of—heaven or hell? And that love, is it love of life or love of death? It is not easy to answer these questions. They all come together in another question: who is Fuensanta?

In a book that is both irritating and enticing in its bristling richness of questions and hypotheses, Denis de Rougemont posits an idea that at first view seems extreme: "The passion of love, glorified by myth, was really at the date of its appearance in the twelfth century a *religion*, in the broad sense of that term, and, specifically, a *Christian heresy*."[6] I confess, not before overcoming considerable resistance and reservation, that I have become almost completely an adherent to this idea. The heresy to which de Rougemont refers is the Manichaeism of the Cathari. The passion of love (or, as the French say, love-passion, something not at all the same as either passionate love or erotic passion) was the archetype of the Provençal poets, and since then it has continued to inspire almost all the imaginative works of the West, the loftiest as well

6. Denis de Rougemont, *L'amour et l'occident*, 2d ed. (Paris, 1956).

as the most vulgar. To the troubadours we owe not only the invention of the basic forms of European lyricism, but also the concept of courtly love, the origin of our image of woman and of passion. De Rougemont contends that the metaphysic implicit in the rhetoric of the troubadours is none other than that of Manichaeism. In fact, both these spiritual movements appeared in the same place sometime in the eleventh century. I do not see how one could dissociate them without breaking the historical unity of a civilization.

It would be excessive to enlarge upon the similarities that the Swiss writer finds between the poems of the Provençals and the beliefs of the Cathari. It is sufficient to point out the most notable: the condemnation of matrimony (the "union of bodies") and the exaltation of a love other than conjugal love, a love that is chaste passion and the promise of reunion beyond this life: woman, the ally of Lucifer and also perpetual temptation to fall into and reproduce matter, is also, as the Lady of courtly love, the immaterial site of spiritual union. The feminine principle, the Lady, is the image of our own soul or, to make use of modern vocabulary, the projection of our own psyche, our anima. A particle of God fallen into the world, a prisoner of the flesh, the soul struggles to free itself from the body and return to the spirit. The soul wishes to be reunited with its anima, that is, with itself. What the lover seeks in the beloved is his lost identity. Sufism, a form of Persian mysticism that is almost surely one of the Oriental roots of courtly love, calls this glorious particle of the soul "angel." In the Mazdean tradition, on the third day of a man's death his angel comes forth to meet him "as a *maiden* of resplendent beauty and says to him, 'I am you yourself.' "[7] But if the man has sinned against his soul, if he has stained his image, he confronts a "monstrous or disfigured apparition, a reflection of his fall."

This little digression responds, albeit indirectly, to the questions provoked by the question of "El sueño de los guantes negros." López Velarde's two loves correspond exactly with the Lady of the Provençal poems. Both real loves blend—or rather dissolve—into the figure of the dead and resuscitated beloved, "the prisoner of the Valley of Mex-

7. Denis de Rougemont, *Comme toi-même* (Paris, 1961).

ico." But this Fuensanta is no longer the provincial love; rather, she is López Velarde's image. She is not an archetype in the sense that the Lady was for the Provençal poets or Beatrice for Dante. The image of a divided and stained conscience, Fuensanta is everything the poet wished and did not wish to be. If she is the Death that conquers death, she is also one who hides her true identity in the prudence of those black gloves.

López Velarde seeks his true being in her image, but when he finds that image he does not recognize himself in it. There is an insuperable distance between Fuensanta and himself. That distance is not physical but moral. The enigma is made more clear if one sees that those gloves conceal an *imperfection*. It is precisely that imperfection that tempts and seduces the poet. And it is possible to know what that tempting imperfection consists of. López Velarde discovered it early in his youth, before his full realization of carnal passions. That poem I cited earlier, "El adiós," describes a scene that is a burlesque allegory: at the moment of separation, Fuensanta leads the poet toward the door; she carries in "her fragile hands" a light that is a "replica of the gospel":

> *but scarcely have they reached the threshold*
> *when—be it the sigh of a soul in torment*
> *or a breath from the spirit of evil—*
> *a gust of air snuffs out the candle.*

Irony alters the image. The intrusion of the critical consciousness undermines Fuensanta's psychic reality as it accentuates her physical reality. Irony does not spring from Fuensanta's body, but from awareness that she has a body. Irony is the devil, the breath of the fallen spirit. As he contemplates that image of his lacerated soul, the poet steps forward and then steps back. He loves that cleft but it also repels him. He is in love with his own laceration. Fuensanta's imperfection is a reflection of the fatal passion that holds him, like Quevedo centuries before him,

> *to the abyss*
> *where I became enamored of myself.*

The abyss of matter in its crude state or of the fallen spirit? Above all, the abyss of self-love. Love that does not know itself since it does not know the other. Thus, alive or dead, here or in the hereafter, Fuensanta is inaccessible. Even had she not been the reflection of a soul struggling against itself (like the souls of all moderns), Fuensanta would have been inaccessible: she was an image. And a stained image. López Velarde is condemned to eternal pursuit, and every time he approaches this woman he must interpose between her image and her being the equivocal reality of those gloves. Emblem of prohibition, the irony of the gloves defends López Velarde from himself (from the unreality of his passion or from the unreality of his soul?). That is his drama. The drama of his first love and of his second, the drama of all his passions, of passion itself: he loved love, the image, more than a real, present, and mortal being. The mystery of the gloves is not a psychological enigma: it is the lost secret—found and lost again—of a spiritual tradition. His passion is not dramatic, as Villaurrutia said and others have since repeated: his drama is *passion.*

López Velarde's dualism is shown with incisive clarity in a much-quoted but little-understood text, "La derrota de la palabra" [The defeat of the word]. In it he contends that his soul is a distant, though inseparable, part of his person. It is, in one way, his feminine half, and in another it is the immortal portion of his being. Thus, he identifies his soul with his second love: she, the incomparable sibyl, is his own soul, his true identity. Like the Provençal ladies, she lives "alone in a craggy castle." She is a cruel lover: "She demands a bedchamber solitude and silence. I long to expel from myself any word, any syllable, not born of the combustion of my bones . . . because in my convulsed soul there is an urgency to dance the religious and voluptuous dance of an Asiatic ritual. And the dancer will not crush on my lips her nudity and her frenzy so long as she hears me stammer one idle syllable." These sentences are always cited as an example of López Velarde's literary doctrine. And so they are, except that his aesthetic is inseparable from his vital quest. To see his quest as something isolated or separated from his real and spiritual life is to mutilate it. The identification between soul and beloved, constant in López Velarde, is the essential element of the concept of love among the Provençal poets and, following them, what distinguishes our idea of love from that of other civilizations.

At the risk of seeming prolix I have no recourse but to enumerate through their various metamorphoses some of the similarities between Fuensanta and the lady of tradition: the secret or symbolic name; inaccessibility (the "unknown princess" of Jaufré Rudel, the provincial girl who is a perpetual adieu, the sibyl); the obstacle (marriage, illness, separation, and especially the body and the awareness that in the body lies the fall: the sword that Tristan and Isolde voluntarily interpose between themselves; the black gloves); the lady as spiritual guide (Beatrice and all her descendants); union after death (from the Provençal poets to the moderns: Nerval's Aurélia, Novalis's Sophie); the confusion between the language of divine love and human love; the hermetic metaphor; the love philters (cabala, witchcraft, or simple intoxication, loss of will; they all signify: I am not I, it is another who speaks in me, an unknown force moves me); the beloved as angel of death, image of the liberation of the spirit; the universe made magnetic by the presence of the lady (or the magical correspondence between the natural and the spiritual orders); sterility (a corollary of the identification of existence with evil); chaste love that does not stand in the way of the search for carnal pleasure (a consequence of the divisive separation between matter and spirit: the pederasty of various Provençal poets, the ardent passions of Dante, Quevedo's sprees, and in López Velarde the "doleful duality / of Ligeia's staring-eyed martyrdom / and Zoraida's bissextile sensuality"); the absolute and inalterable fidelity to the lady, even though other love affairs intervene (for the same Manichaean reason); the voyage or the pilgrimage (search for the distant lady, descents into hell, voyages to the interior of the consciousness, love of open spaces, returns to infancy and the house of one's birth: the archetype here, the *Divine Comedy*); and, finally, the projection of the innermost "I" into the figure of the beloved, the search for identity. The phrase with which the angel receives the dead in the Persian legend is tirelessly repeated throughout the whole of European poetry, at times as laceration, as in Baudelaire's "Madrigal triste" [Madrigal of sorrow]: in the "unwholesome night," the beloved, a "damned soul," says to him: "I am your equal, oh my king." All these elements blend into aspiration for the spirit's immortality—or its dissolution. So this is the mystery of passion, the enigma of love: the anima we seek in this world and beyond, is it death? Soul, beloved, death: "I no longer know where you end and where I begin: we are . . . the same knot of love."

I do not suggest that López Velarde embraced the religion of a twelfth-century sect. That would be grotesque and would scarcely be worth clarifying. Furthermore, love-passion is a heresy that does not know it is heresy. And even if it were not, if the affinities between the Cathari and courtly love were only coincidence, it is evident that the work of our poet belongs to the central tradition of Occidental poetry. Only in the light of that tradition is his anguish—the continuous oscillation of his soul, always on the verge of drowning, always miraculously suspended on the wave—revealed for what it truly is: a conflict of the spirit, not the disordered movement of a sick consciousness. The famous formula—López Velarde is the poet of eroticism and death—although it is intended to embrace a great deal, really says nothing. It is a commonplace of modern psychology. Eroticism, death, and love occupy the heart of his poetry because López Velarde assumes, in his life and in his work, a spiritual tradition that since its beginnings has been swayed by the mysterious relationships of those three words. The other definitions—poet of the provinces and poet of sentimental love—sin at the opposite extreme by reducing him to a picturesque specificity or by converting him into the spirit of foolishness. Provincial, sentimental, erotic, or funereal, López Velarde is a poet of love, in the almost religious sense of the expression "the passion of love." His work is situated on the main road of a tradition initiated in Provence, in which certain names serve as points of sensitive radiation: Dante and Petrarch, the Spanish baroque and the English metaphysical poets, the German Romantics, Baudelaire and the French Symbolists. And that poetic road is also the road of passion; in every period it has given us an image of woman. López Velarde is more than a poetic temperament: he is a tradition.

He never hid from himself the fact that sterility was not the true remedy for the sin of fecundity. To refuse to contribute to the propagation of evil is not to do good; more accurately, it is desertion. As he listens to the repeated throbbing of his heart he feels "the remorseful tenderness of a father" who senses "the lifebeat of a blind son in his arms." And in a strange fit of anger and desperation he dreams of tearing that son from his breast and raising him high in triumph so he may "know the day." This evocation of the Aztec sacrifice has a most unusual effect, since López Velarde was neither very fond of, nor knew much about, our indigenous past. Rather this is a case of the true eruption of a world buried in the depths of his being. The subconscious memory of the ancient rite is made more precise in the last stanza of the poem. From the summit—of the mountain or the pyramid?—he will hurl his heart into the "solar bonfire":

> *Thus shall I extirpate the cancer of my cruel exhaustion,*
> *I shall be impassive to the east and to the west,*
> *I shall attend with a depraved smile*
> *the ineptitudes of an inept culture,*
> *and in my heart shall be a flame that will invest it*
> *with the symphonic incense of the celestial sphere.*

Only on a few occasions was López Velarde a violent poet, and never was he so violent as in this poem. But the purification by fire, the return to the elements, could only grant him impassivity, never immortality. To throw his heart into the blaze was to annihilate the spirit, to dissolve it in cosmic indifference.

The temptation represented by the return to original chaos does not present itself again in other poems, at least not with such intensity. A more kindred course opens to him. In one of his best prose poems, "Obra maestra," he says that his son must be a spiritual creature, a consciousness from his consciousness, perfect and invulnerable: "He exists in the transcendental glory where neither his shoulders nor his brow shall be oppressed by the weight of horror, of sanctity, of beauty, or of loathsomeness . . . He lives in me like the absolute angel, a fellow to the human species. Created from rectitude, affliction, intransigence, from a fury for pleasure and abnegation, the son I have never had is my true masterpiece." Biological sterility is resolved into spiritual fecundity.

His mission is the creation of a son, not human, although resembling man: the absolute angel. This paragraph corresponds, almost letter for letter, with the doctrines of the Cathari and the concept of the angel in Persian mysticism. To identify the spiritual son with his work, as earlier he identified the son of his flesh with his heart, is to "transfigure the fall into flight . . . joining together at the same time the ascension and the assumption."

The titles of four of his books all allude to the heart: *La sangre devota, El minutero, El son del corazón,* and *Zozobra.* The heart, as symbol and as reality, is the sun/center of his work and all other elements of his poetry rotate within its light or its shadow. His aesthetic is the "heart's impulse"; his language, "the sound of the heart"; the beloved, "the blood's elect"; the spectacle of the world, alluring and terrible, causes him to say that "everything asks me for blood"; Fuensanta's heart is of "snow and theology," his own—obscurantist, rash, devoted to the Virgin of Guadalupe—is a magnet, a grove that speaks, an Andalusian pond, an all-possessing pontiff, a scale, an anthill of rancor, a clock of agonies. With the obsession of a cardiac patient he repeats the words asphyxia, embrace, suffocation. He hears the blood and its cruel swelling in the noise of the sea. Although many of these expressions denote a real physiological anguish, it would be absurd to reduce them to a maniacal preoccupation with the body.

The heart is time. Clock of blood, its ticking contains the paradox of the instant by being the highest point of the temporal tide, the extreme intensity of time, and in the same movement its annihilation. The instant reconciles the oppositions of which temporal succession is made (past and future) into a dense present: that plenitude is a tearing and ripping: as it looses its hold on the before, the now floats in a vacuum, perpetual anguish, imminence of fall. The analogy between the instant and the heart also embraces love: systole and diastole, ascent and descent, union and dispersion: a pulsation above the abyss. López Velarde inhabits the instant because he chose the passion of love. He was loyal to his heart. As in the case of paternity without flesh-and-blood sons, that loyalty is transfigured by poetry. Time, without ceasing, must overtake itself; love, unchanging, must be a fixed star. His work's purpose is to achieve the mutation of the instant into spiritual time, of volatile love into fidelity unto death. Only in his work will the arrow of the instant, which is love or disaffection, "be miraculous, because we shall be so swift that we will achieve the shooting and the receiving of the shot in a single act." In the poem the poet will, in the same instant, be the archer, the victim, and the arrow.

All those who have approached López Velarde's poetry have pointed out the frequency of the imagery of ebb and flow, coming and going: the pendulum, the scale, the swing, the trapeze. The sensation of emptiness and vertigo is generally allied to those evocations. And death is ever present, the basis of eternal fluctuation. Uranga has seen in this oscillation the image of contingency, the origin of Mexican "insecurity." Phillips confines himself to literary criticism, carefully examining for several pages this "imaginative predilection." Villaurrutia recognizes in the figure of the trapeze the duality that rules the poet's spirit. It is the sign of a soul divided between opposites. True, but one must add something else. López Velarde does not live out his conflict passively. His work is not only a description of the contradictory movement of his soul; it is also an attempt to create himself, a search for a state that will reconcile contradiction. For that reason he chooses the instant and the work of art, love and fidelity: all of them. The poem transfigures the instant and thus redeems it. The image of the trapeze, an emblem of the instant, shows us the way to reconciliation. The trapeze and its oscillation contain two anguished notes: suspension over the void, and repetition. They are the unfinished and the unending; human life, never fixed, never stable—until life ceases. The poem does not immobilize the trapeze; rather, it gives meaning to its mechanical movement. The work is a double response to the immobility of death and to the oscillation of life.

In one poem, "El candil," López Velarde at last believes he has found repose in movement. A lantern in the shape of a ship, hanging from the dome of a Mexican-Spanish church, fixed in the interior space of the temple, this lamp is the transfiguration of the trapeze. Thus it is converted into his personal emblem. A symbol of voyage and return, the lamp/ship is also a heart beating in the religious night: "God sees its pulsing." A metamorphosis of the trapeze and its quotidian drama, of the heart and the instant, the lamp is the winking of a light with no office except that of adoration:

> *Oh lantern, oh ship: before the altar*
> *we fulfill, in a recondite duet,*
> *one single mission: to venerate.*

The symbol of the lamp is one example of the mission López Velarde assigns to poetry. Fuensanta is another. If the instant is oscillation, eroticism is fluctuation. The beloved gives meaning and unity to the erotic experience. The death woman is the fixed star: perhaps it disappeared thousands of years ago, but its splendor guides one's tortuous pilgrimage as the reliquary of the host guides the navigation of the lamp/ship. There is a magnet that attracts opposing elements, a center: the heart, concord. To seek that center was his destiny as a poet. Although he may not have encountered it, he left us the trail of his quest: his poems. The meaning of his work will escape us if we fail to recognize that it is a search for, and at times an encounter with—not himself, but something I dare not call God, or the truth beyond, or the spirit, in spite of the fact that it has all those names. Perhaps these phrases are too vague; for that reason I prefer to use one of López Velarde's expressions: "the sanctity of the person." A state—no matter how sad or forsaken the creature's condition—of reconciliation with oneself and, simultaneously, detachment from oneself.

The opposite of the insensibility that eroticism proposes to us is active contemplation. The libertine ends in indifference or apathy because he began by feeling indifference for his fellows. As a man and as a poet López Velarde's attempt goes in the opposite direction: his work begins with his passionate interest in things and in men and particularly in everything that traditional poetry had judged insignificant or trivial. The tie he established between the world and his person is of amorous inclination: the embrace, the cordial metaphor. But the embrace is a bridge over the void. Once the bedazzlement of the erotic lightning flash has passed, the embrace is succeeded by a state of contemplation become communion with the things around us, whether night or light, nature or spirit. This attitude is reflected in some of the poems in *Zozobra* and *El son del corazón.* This direction, interrupted perhaps by his death, was never wholly developed. It does not matter: he left us several poems that point the way. One of them is "Todo." The poem begins as a declaration, half-ironic and half-exalted, of his aesthetic, of his beliefs, and of the meaning of his poetic mission. His "somnambulistic and pungent voice" is the native-born voice of cinnamon (an admirable definition of his poetry and of the place it occupies in the tradition of our language: enormous smallness); his time is the instant: he lives in "the heart of every minute"; the realities designated by the words flesh and spirit seem laughable and absurd to him: on the other hand, if he says "I" his faith never vacillates. This I, humble and sacred, whose emblem is the lamp, is untouchable and invulnerable. Because of it he denies neither himself nor his appetites; because of it his interior discord is resolved into the unity of his person. Even so, that dispersed I is conscious of its disperseness and thus, "in spite of the moralist besieging it, and above the farce," *his person is holy.* Loyalty to one's heart becomes saintliness when we succeed in perceiving in its beating the harmony of opposites. His person is neither selfish nor "committed." In total leisure, his only activity is imagination:

> *Although it is the poet's lot*
> *to live passively,*
> *I live the formidable life*
> *of all men and women.*

The sympathy he feels for his fellow beings should not be confused with the desire to guide or reform that many preach today, with as much hypocrisy as cruelty. His love is love, not tyrannical pedagogy. And it is a love that does not stop with man. His person is holy (in its contradiction and in its fall) because in it throbs a "pontiff" who consecrates every existing thing. Although he owns nothing, his heart gives shelter to "dolorous nature and its three kingdoms . . ." And suddenly he suspends this enumeration, he abandons the tone of reflective confidence, and he writes two of the most beautiful and enigmatic lines written in Spanish in this century. In spite of their hermeticism, their spiritual meaning seems so evident to me that I deem any explanation useless and rash. These lines express the experience of unity in diversity and contradict the frenzy of passion with the serenity of compassion. They represent, not indifference, but the loving gaze of one who contemplates the differences between creatures and their final identity. López Velarde says he is stirred

> *by the ignorance of the snow*
> *and the wisdom of the hyacinth.*

M.S.P.

The Rider of the Air

[PARIS, 1960]

A telegram from Mexico City told me of the death of Alfonso Reyes. The news seemed unreal to me, as if it announced the death of another person. I knew that he had been ill for years and that whenever he recovered it was only to fall ill again. What I did not know, or had forgotten, was that death, while always expected, is always unexpected. The last time I saw him, six months ago, just before I left Mexico, he told me: "Perhaps we won't have another conversation. There isn't much time left to me." And with a glance he pointed toward his books. I have forgotten what I replied; no doubt it was one of those vague phrases in which, not without hypocrisy, we try to calm both the anxiety of the ill and our own secret fear of death. I remember that I felt a ridiculous shame, as if my own good health were something indiscreet and little deserved. Reyes noticed my confusion, changed the topic, and happily guided me through the thickets of hermetic poetry.

It was an admirable proof of moral health. In an epoch deafened by screams, an ill man, closed up in his library, almost without hope of being heard, bends over a forgotten text and weighs images and pauses, rhythms and silences, in a delicate verbal scale. In a world that has almost completely lost the sense of form, to the extent that the manufactured phrase, after conquering newspapers, parliaments, and universities, becomes the favorite means of expression of poets and novelists, the love that Reyes had for language, for its problems and its mysteries, is something more than an example: it is a miracle. I rarely found Reyes so lucid, so clear and lightninglike, so daring and so reticent—in a word, so alive—as that night when he spoke to me, between occasional whiffs of oxygen, about the delights and dangers of Lycophron and Gracián. Want of humanity, social insensitivity, lack of a sense of history? I would say love of life in an age that venerates not so much

Moser 1975

death as the *absence of life*. The cult of death is an archaic superstition. We, the moderns, adore the bloodless abstraction and the shapeless number: neither life nor death. Reyes's love, his loves, were different: love of form, love of life. Form is the embodiment of life, the instant in which life makes a covenant with itself.

No, we are not made for death, and Alfonso Reyes—"knight-errant of May," the solar month, as he says in one of his poems—was the man least disposed, philosophically, to die. Not because of a sterile rebellion against the idea of death but because to him dying did not seem an *idea*, that is, a reason, something possessing meaning. He never made a philosophy of death, as so many writers in our language have done. Instead, he saw it as a negation, a definitive refutation of the very idea of philosophy. He accepted it, not without irony, as one more proof of cosmic insanity. He was not wrong: death is the fruit, the *natural* consequence, of life, and as such it is not an accident. Nevertheless, it is the great accident, the only accident. And this—its being contingent and necessary—makes it still more enigmatic. Death is the universal contradiction.

Reyes, the lover of measure and proportion, a man for whom everything. including action and passion, had to resolve itself in equilibrium, knew that we are surrounded by chaos and silence. Formlessness, whether as a vacuum or as a brute presence, lies in wait for us. But he never tried to put instinct in chains, to suppress the dark side of man. He did not preach the equivocal virtues of repression, either in the realm of ethics or in that of aesthetics, and even less so in politics. Wakefulness and sleep, blood and thought, friendship and solitude, the city and women: each part and each one must be given its own. The portion of instinct is no less sacred than that of the spirit. And what are the limits between one and another? Everything communicates. Man is a vast and delicate alchemy. The human action par excellence is transmutation, which makes light from shadow, the word from a cry, dialogue from the elemental quarrel.

His love for Hellenic culture, the reverse of his indifference toward Christianity, was something more than an intellectual inclination. He saw Greece as a model because what its poets and philosophers revealed to him was something that was already within him and that, thanks to them, received a name and an answer: the terrible powers of hubris and the means of controlling them. Greek literature did not show him a philosophy, a moral, a "what should be." Rather, it showed him being itself in all its welter, in its alternately creative and destructive rhythms. The Greek norms, Jaeger says, are a manifestation of the inherent lawfulness of the cosmos; the movement of being, its dialectic. On several occasions Reyes wrote that tragedy is the highest and most perfect form of poetry and ethics because, in tragedy, lack of proportion finds at last its strict measure and is thus purified and redeemed. Passion is creative when it finds its form. To Reyes, form was not an envelopment or an abstract measure, but rather the instant of reconciliation in which discord is transformed into harmony. The true name of this harmony is liberty: fatality ceases to be an imposition from without and becomes an intimate and voluntary acceptance. Ethics and aesthetics are intertwined in Reyes's thinking: liberty is an aesthetic act, that is, it is the moment of concord between passion and form, vital energy and the human measure; at the same time, form and measure constitute an ethical dimension because they rescue us from excess, which is chaos and destruction.

These ideas, scattered through many of his pages and books, are the invisible blood that animates Reyes's most perfect poetic work: *Ifigenia cruel* [Cruel Iphigenia]. Perhaps it is not necessary to remark that this poem is, among many other things, a symbol of a personal drama and the answer that the poet meant to give it. His family belonged to the *ancien régime*. His father had been minister of war and his elder brother, the jurist Bernardo Reyes, was a university professor and a renowned political polemicist. Both were enemies of Madero's revolutionary government. His father died in the attack on the National Palace and his brother, when the revolutionaries triumphed, fled to Spain and constantly attacked the new regime from there. Hence Alfonso Reyes's situation was not very different from that of Iphigenia: his brother reminded him that vengeance is a filial duty and that to refuse to follow the voice of the blood is to condemn oneself to serving a bloodthirsty goddess—Artemis in the one case, the Mexican Revolution in the other.

The poem is something more, of course, than an expression of this personal conflict; as a vision of woman and as a meditation on liberty, *Ifigenia cruel* is one of the most complete and perfect works in modern Spanish American poetry.

Reyes chose the second part of the myth. At the moment when Iphigenia is to die at Aulis, Artemis, to placate the wrath of the wind, exchanges her body for that of a hind and takes her to Tauris. There she consecrates her as a priestess of her temple: Iphigenia is to immolate every stranger who arrives at the island. One day she recognizes Orestes among the strangers whom a shipwreck has cast up on the shore. Destiny, the law of the breed, wins out: brother and sister flee, after robbing the statue of the goddess, and return to Attica. Reyes introduces here a fundamental change in the story, one that does not appear in either Euripides or Goethe: Iphigenia has lost her memory. She does not know who she is or where she comes from. She only knows that she is "a mass of naked rage." As a virgin without origins, who "sprouted like a fungus on the stones of the temple," bound to the bloody stone from the beginning of beginnings, a virgin with neither a past nor a future, Iphigenia is blind movement without self-awareness, condemned to repeat itself endlessly. The appearance of Orestes breaks the enchantment; his words penetrate her petrified consciousness and she passes gradually from recognition of the "other"—the unknown and delirious brother, the always remote fellow human being—to the rediscovery of her lost identity. Reyes seems to suggest that, in order to be ourselves, we must recognize the existence of others. When she recovers her memory, Iphigenia recovers her self. She is in possession of her own being because she knows who she is: the magic virtue of the name. Memory has given her back her consciousness, and, in so doing, it has granted her her freedom. She is no longer possessed by Artemis, no longer "bound to the trunk of her self," and can now choose. Her choice—and here the difference from the traditional version is even more significant—is unexpected: Iphigenia decides to remain in Tauris. Two words— "two words that are empty shells: I refuse"—are enough to change the whole course of fate in one vertiginous instant. By this act she renounces the memory she has just recovered, says "No" to destiny, to her family and origins, to the laws of the earth and the blood. And, beyond that, she renounces her own self. That negation engenders a new self-affirmation. In renouncing her self, she chooses. And this act, free above all others, an affirmation of the sovereignty of the spirit, a shining of liberty, is a second birth. Iphigenia is now the daughter of her own self.

Reyes's poem, which was written in 1923, not only anticipates many contemporary preoccupations but also contains—in code, in a condensed language that partakes of the hardness of stone and the bitterness of the sea, skillful and savage at one and the same time—all the later evolution of his spirit. All of Reyes—the best, the freest, the least trammeled —is in this work. There are even a secret wink, a malicious aside for the delectation of the knowing, and anachronisms and a pointing of the intelligence toward other lands and other times. There is erudition, but there are also grace, imagination, and a painful lucidity. Iphigenia, her knife, and her goddess, an immense stone fashioned by blood, allude simultaneously to pre-Columbian cults and "the eternal feminine"; the sonnet in Orestes's monologue is a double homage to Góngora and to the Spanish theater of the seventeenth century; the shadow of Segismundo sometimes obscures Iphigenia's face; at other times, the virgin speaks enigmas like the "Hérodiade" [Herodias] of Mallarmé or gropes with her thoughts like "La jeune parque" [The young Fate]; Euripides and Goethe, the Catholic concept of free will, the rhythmic experiments of Modernism, even Mexican themes (universalism and nationalism) and the family quarrel, all are brought together here with admirable naturalness. There is nothing too much because there is nothing lacking. True, he never again wrote a poem so solid and so aerial in its architecture, so rich in meanings, but the best pages of his prose are an impassioned meditation on the mystery of Iphigenia, the virgin liberty.

The enigma of liberty is also that of woman. Artemis is pure and cruel divinity: she is moon and water, the goddess of the third millennium before Christ, the tamer, the huntress, and the fatal enchantress. Iphigenia is just barely a human manifestation of that pallid and terrible deity, who runs through the nocturnal woods followed by a blood-thirsty pack of hounds. Artemis is a pillar, the primordial tree, archetype of the column as the grove is mythical model of the temple. That pillar is the center of the world:

The stars dance about you.
Alas for the world if you weaken, Goddess!

Artemis is virgin and impenetrable: "Who glimpsed the hermetic
mouth of your two vertical legs?" Eye of stone, mouth of stone—but
"the roots of her fingers suck up the red cubes of the sacrifice at each
moon." She is cliff, pillar, statue, still water, but she is also the mad
rush of the wind through the trees. Artemis alternately seeks and refuses incarnation, the meeting with the other, the adversary and complement of her being. The carnal embrace is mortal combat.

Eroticism—in the modern meaning of the term—is always veiled in
Reyes's work. Irony moderates the shout; sensuality sweetens the
mouth's terrible grimace; tenderness transforms the claw into a caress.
Love is a battle, not a slaughter. Reyes does not deny the omnipotence
of desire but—without closing his eyes to the contradictory nature of
pleasure—he seeks a new equilibrium. In *Ifigenia cruel* and other writ-
ings desire wears the armor of death, but in his more numerous and
more personal works his cordial temperament—melancholy, tenderness,
saudade ("nostalgia")—calms the blood and its hornets. Reyes's epi-
cureanism is neither an aesthetics nor a morality: it is a vital defense, a
manly remedy. A pact: no surrender, but also no war without quarter.
In one of his youthful poems, much more complex than it seems at a
first reading, he says that in his imagination he identifies the flower
(which is a magic flower: the sleeping poppy) with woman and confesses his fear:

I tremble, let the day not dawn
in which you turn into a woman!

The flower, like woman, hides a menace. Both provoke dreams, delirium, and madness. Both bewitch—which is to say, paralyze—the spirit.
To free oneself from the virgin Iphigenia's knife and the menace of the
flower, there is no known exorcism except love, sacrifice—which is, *always*, a transfiguration. In Reyes's work the sacrifice is not consummated and love is an oscillation between solitude and companionship.
Woman ("bound up in the hour—free, although she gives herself, and

alien") is ours for only an instant in reality. And, in the memory, forever, like nostalgia:

> *Thank you, Río, thank you,*
> *Solitude and companionship,*
> *Smooth water for all anguish,*
> *Harbor in every storm.*

Pact, agreement, equilibrium: these words appear frequently in Reyes's work and define one of the central directions of his thought. Some critics, not content with accusing him of Byzantinism (there are criticisms that, on certain lips, are really eulogies), have reproached him for his moderation. A spirit of moderation? I refuse to believe it, at least in the simple way in which simplistic minds want to see it. A spirit in search of equilibrium, an aspiration toward measure, and also a grand universal appetite, a desire to embrace everything, the most remote disciplines as well as the most distant epochs. Not to repress contradictions but to integrate them in broader affirmations; to order particulars of knowledge into general—but always provisional—schemes. Curiosity and prudence: every day we discover that there is still something we need to know, and, if it is true that everything has been thought, it is also true that nothing has been thought. No one has the last word. It is easy to see the uses and risks of this attitude. On the one hand, it irritates people with categorical minds who have the truth clenched in their fists. On the other, an excess of knowledge sometimes makes us timid and weakens our confidence in our spontaneous impulses. Reyes was not paralyzed by erudition because he defended himself with an invincible weapon: humor. To laugh at one's self, to laugh at one's own knowledge, is a way of growing lighter.

Góngora says: "The sea is not deaf: erudition is deceptive." Reyes was not always free from the deceptions of that sort of erudition that causes us to see yesterday's madness in today's novelties. Besides, his temperament led him to flee from extremes. This explains, perhaps, his reserve when considering those civilizations and spirits that express what could be called sublime exaggeration. (I am thinking of the Orient and of pre-Columbian America but also of Novalis and Rimbaud.) I will always lament his coldness toward the great adventure of contemporary art and poetry. German Romanticism, Dostoevsky, modern poetry (in its more daring forms), Kafka, Lawrence, Joyce, and some others were territories that he traversed with an explorer's valor but without amorous passion. And even in this I am afraid of being unjust, because how can one forget his fondness for Mallarmé, one of the very poets who most clearly embodies the modern artist's thirst for the absolute? He was blamed for the mildness of his public life, and some said that on occasion his character was not of the same stature as his talent and the circumstances around him. It is true that sometimes he kept still; it is also true that he never screeched as did many of his contemporaries. If he never suffered persecution, he also never persecuted anyone. He was not a party man; he was not fascinated by force or numbers; he did not believe in leaders; he never published noisy statements of support; he would not renounce his past, his thoughts, or his work; he did not confess nor employ autocriticism; he was not "converted." His indecisions, even his weaknesses—because he had them— were changed into strengths and nourished his freedom. This tolerant and affable man lived and died a heterodoxist, outside all churches and parties.

Reyes's work is disconcerting not only in its quantity but also in the variety of the matters it deals with. Yet it is the farthest thing from being a scattering. Everything tends toward a synthesis, including that part of his literary work made up of his annotations and summaries of other people's books. In an epoch of discord and uniformity—two faces of the same coin—Reyes postulates a will for harmony, that is, for an order that does not exclude the singularity of the parts. His interest in political and social utopias and his continuous meditation on the duties of the Spanish American "intelligence" have the same origin as his fondness for Hellenistic studies, the philosophy of history, and comparative literature. He seeks in everything the individual trait, the personal variation; and he always succeeds in placing this singularity in a vaster harmony. But harmony, agreement, and equilibrium are words that do not define him clearly. "Concord," a spiritual word, fits him better. He is more worthy of it. Concord is not concession, pact, or compromise, but a dynamic game of opposites, concordance of the being and the other, reconciliation between movement and repose, coincidence of passion and form. The surge of life, the coming and going of the blood, the hand that opens and closes: to give and to receive and to give again. Concord, a central, vital word. Not brain, not belly, not sex, not cave-man's jaw: heart.

Death is the only irrefutable proposition, the only undeniable reality. At the same time, perhaps because of the excess of reality it manifests, because of the brutality with which it tells us that presence is absence, death gives an air of unreality to everything we see, not excluding the very corpse whose wake we are attending. Everything is and is not. Our ultimate reality is nothing but a definitive unreality. It could be said, modifying slightly a line by Borges: "Death, scrupulous of unreality." Reyes is here and is not here. I see him and I do not see him. As in his poem,

> *The rider of the air passes by,*
> *mounted on his fresh mare,*
> *and does not pass by: he is in the shadows*
> *clinking his spurs.*

Reyes still gallops. His arms—the hand and the intelligence, the sun and the heart—gleam in the darkness.

L.K.

II.

Robert Frost

E. E. Cummings

Saint-John Perse

Antonio Machado

Jorge Guillén

B. MOSER · 1975

Visit to a Poet

[VERMONT, 1945]

After walking along the road for twenty minutes in the three-o'clock sun, I finally came to the bend. I turned right and began to climb the slope. At intervals the trees bordering the path afforded a little coolness. There was water running among grasses in a brook. The sand creaked under my shoes. The sun was everywhere. The air smelled of hot, thirsty green weeds. Not a leaf stirred on the trees. Above them, a few clouds rested heavily, anchored in a windless blue gulf. A bird sang. I halted: "It would be much better to lie down under the elm. The sound of water is worth more than all the words of poets." And I walked on for another ten minutes. When I reached the farm, several blond children were playing around a birch tree. I asked them about the owner, and without stopping their game they pointed toward the top of the hill and said, "He's up there in the cabin." I started walking again. I climbed through tall weeds that came up to my knees. When I reached the top I could see out over all of the small valley: the blue mountains, the brook, the luminous green fields and the woods beyond them. The wind began to blow, and everything swayed, almost joyously. I approached the cabin. It was an old, unpainted little wooden house that had turned gray with age. There were no curtains at the windows, so I shoved through the weeds and peered in. The old man was inside sitting in an easy chair. A woolly dog rested beside him. When he saw me, he stood up and gestured that I should go around. I took a turn and found him waiting for me at the door of the cabin. The dog jumped up and down to welcome me. We went through an entryway and into a small room: unpolished wooden floor, two chairs, a blue easy chair, another reddish one, a desk with a few books, a small table with papers and letters. Three or four pictures on the walls, none of them remarkable. We sat down.

"It's hot, eh? Would you like to have a beer?"

"Yes, I think I would. I have been walking for half an hour and I feel tired."

We drank the beer slowly. With his open white shirt—is there anything cleaner than a clean white shirt?—his innocent and ironical blue eyes, his philosopher's head and farmer's hands, he appeared an ancient sage, one of those who prefer to see the world from their place of retirement. But there was nothing ascetic about his appearance, only a virile sobriety. There he was in his cabin, retired from the world, not in order to renounce it but to contemplate it better. He was not a hermit and his hilltop was not a rock in the desert. The bread he ate had not been brought to him by the three ravens, he had bought it himself at the village store.

"This is a really beautiful spot. It almost seems unreal. The landscape is very different from ours, it is more suited to the eyes of man. And the distances, too, they are better made for our legs."

"My daughter has told me the landscapes in your country are very dramatic."

"Nature is hostile down there. Besides, we are few and weak. The landscape swallows men up, and there is always the danger of being changed into a cactus."

"I've been told the people are still for hours on end, without doing anything at all."

"In the late afternoon you can see them sitting motionless along the edge of the road or at the entrance to the village."

"Is that how they do their thinking?"

"It is a country that will turn to stone some day. The trees and plants are tending toward stone, the same as the people. And the animals, too, the dogs and coyotes and snakes. There are birds made of baked clay and it is very strange to see them fly and hear them sing, because you have not got used to the idea that they are actually birds."

"I'm going to tell you something. When I was fifteen years old I wrote a poem, my first poem. And do you know what the theme was? The Noche Triste. I'd been reading Prescott around then and perhaps my reading made me think of your country. Have you read Prescott?"

"It was one of my grandfather's favorite books, so I read it when I was a child. I would like to read it again."

"I like to reread books too. I'm suspicious of people who don't reread. And of people who read a lot of books. This modern mania seems crazy to me; it only increases the number of pedants. It's better to read a few books well and read them many times."

"A friend of mine tells me they have invented a method for increasing one's reading speed. I believe they are thinking of using it in the schools."

"They're crazy. What they ought to teach people is how to read slowly. And not to move around so much. Do you know why they invent all these things? Out of fear. People are afraid to pause over things, because that compromises them. That's why they run away from the land and go to the cities. They're afraid of being alone."

"Yes, the world is full of fear."

"And the ones in power take advantage of that fear. The individual has never been so despised and authority so revered."

"Of course, it is easier not to live for oneself, not to decide for oneself. It is even easier to die if you die on someone else's account. We are overwhelmed by fear. There is the fear of the common man, who surrenders to the strong. But there is also the fear of those in power, who don't dare to be alone. They grasp for power out of fear."

"Up here, people leave the land to go to work in factories. And when they come back they don't like the countryside any more. The countryside is difficult. You have to be alert all the time and you're responsible for everything, not just for a part the way you are in a factory."

"Also, the countryside is an experience in solitude. You can't go to the movies, you can't take refuge in a bar."

"Exactly. It's an experience in freedom. It's like poetry. Life is like poetry, when a poet writes a poem. It starts out by being an invitation to the unknown: he writes the first line and doesn't know what comes next. We don't know what's waiting for us in the next line, whether it's poetry or failure. And the poet has that sense of mortal danger in all his adventures."

"There is a decision waiting for us in every line, and we can't get around it by shutting our eyes and letting instinct work by itself. Poetic instinct consists in an alert tension."

"The chance of failure is hiding in every line, every phrase. So is the danger that the whole poem will fail, not just a single line. And that's how life is: we can lose it at any moment. Each moment is a mortal risk. And each instant is a choice."

"You are right. Poetry is an experience in freedom. The poet takes chances, he gambles the whole poem in every line he writes."

"And you can't take it back. Each act, each line, is irrevocable and forever. You're compromised forever in every line. But now people have become irresponsible. No one wants to decide for himself. Like those poets who imitate their predecessors."

"You do not believe in tradition?"

"Yes, but each poet is born to express something of his own. And his first obligation is to deny his ancestors, the rhetoric of earlier poets. When I began writing I found out that the words of the ancients wouldn't serve me. I had to create my own language by myself. And that language, which surprised and bothered some people, was the language of my own people, the language I heard all around me in my childhood and adolescence. I had to wait a long time to find my own words. You have to use everyday language . . ."

"But putting it under a different pressure. As if each word had been created just to express that particular moment. Because there is a certain fatefulness in words. A French writer says that 'images are not sought, they are encountered.' I don't believe he means that chance determines one's writing but that a fated choice brings us to certain words."

"The poet creates his own language. And then he should struggle against that rhetoric. He should never surrender to his own style."

"There are no poetic styles. When a style is reached, literature takes the place of poetry."

"That was the situation in American poetry when I started writing. That's where all my difficulties began, and all my lucky hits. And now maybe it's necessary to struggle against the rhetoric we've created. The world turns around, my friend, and what was up yesterday is down today. You have to scoff a little at all this. You can't take anything too seriously, even ideas. Or, to put it better, it's exactly because we're so serious and passionate that we ought to laugh at ourselves. I don't trust people who don't know how to laugh."

And he laughed with the laugh of a man who has seen it rain, and who has also got wet. We stood up and went outside for a walk. His dog leaped about ahead of us as we went down the slope. After we were outside he said, "Above all, I don't trust people who don't know how to laugh at themselves. Solemn poets, humorless professors, prophets who only know how to howl and harangue. Those kinds of men are dangerous."

"Do you read the moderns?"

"I always read poetry. I like to read what the young poets are writing. And also a few philosophers. But I can't stand novels. I don't think I've ever read a one."

We went on walking. When we reached the farmhouse, the children surrounded us. The poet talked to me now about his childhood, about the years in San Francisco and the return to New England.

"This is my land and I think it's where the nation's roots are. Everything sprang from here. Did you know that the state of Vermont refused to take part in the war against Mexico? Yes, everything sprang from here. The desire to explore the unknown, and the desire to be alone with yourself, they both got started here. And we've got to go back to that if we want to preserve what we are."

"That seems to me very difficult. You people are already so wealthy."

"Years ago, I thought of going to a small country where I wouldn't hear the noise everybody makes. I picked Costa Rica. But while I was getting ready for the trip I found out an American company was doing business even there, and I gave up. That's why I'm here, in New England."

We came to the bend. I looked at my watch: more than two hours had gone by.

"I think I should go. They are waiting for me down there at Bread Loaf."

He reached out his hand to me. "Do you know the way?"

"Yes," I said. And I shook his hand. After I had taken a few steps, I heard his voice: "Come back soon! And, when you get back to New York, write to me. Don't forget."

I replied with a nod. I saw him go up the path, playing with his dog. "And he is seventy years old," I said to myself. As I walked back I remembered another solitary, another visit. "I think Robert Frost would have liked to know Antonio Machado. But how could they have understood each other? The Spaniard could not speak English and this poet knows no Spanish. No matter—they would have smiled at each other. I am sure they would have become friends immediately." I remembered the house at Rocafort, in Valencia, the wild, untended garden, the dusty living room and furniture. And Machado, with a dead cigar in his mouth. The Spaniard was also an elderly sage who had retired from the world and who also knew how to laugh and who was also absent-minded. He enjoyed philosophizing, like the Yankee, not in schools but out on the fringes. Two village sages, the American in his cabin, the Spaniard in his provincial café. Machado, too, professed that he was horrified by solemnity, and he had the same smiling gravity. "Yes, the New Englander has the cleaner shirt, and more trees in his look. But the other had the sadder and finer smile. There is much snow in this man's poems, but there are dust, antiquity, history in the other's. That dust of Castile, that dust of Mexico, which, when you barely touch it, sifts through your fingers . . ."

L.K.

E. E. Cummings

[DELHI, 1965]

I read him for the first time in Berkeley in 1944. He dazzled me. Later, without losing my initial astonishment, I recognized in his work that rare alliance between verbal invention and passionate fatality that distinguishes the poem from the literary fabrication. None of Cummings's so-called extravagances—typography, punctuation, plays on words, syntax in which nouns, adjectives, and even pronouns tend to become verbs—is arbitrary. His poetry is a game that, like all play, obeys a strict logic. And play, like poetry, partakes of the marvelous in that it sets necessity in motion to produce risk or something that resembles it: the unexpected. There is nothing less gratuitous than a composition by Cummings; nothing more surprising. Play and passion. Because Cummings, the great innovator, is a poet of love, and for that reason he is also a poet of indignation. His satires and diatribes against the civilization and morality of his country are no less impassioned— and no less piercing—than his love poems. From the first book to the last, his is a young poetry—which the young very rarely write. It is said that he repeats himself. Perhaps it is true. It has to be added that, if there is no evolution in his work, there is also no descent. In his earliest poems he achieved a perfection that could only be called incandescent if it were not at the same time freshness itself. A springtime of flames.

Cummings's poems are the children of calculation at the service of passion. Has it been noted that passion, in life as much as in art, demands a maximum of artifice for its satisfaction and is never content with reality unless it first transmutes it into symbols? Eroticism tends toward ceremony; love is emblematical; curiosity grows exalted in front of enigmas—among the ancients, both a children's game and a rite of passage. Conundrums, eroticism, love: systems of correspondence, languages in which not only objects, colors, and sounds but also bodies and souls are symbols. We live in a world of signs. All of Cummings's images

MOSER 1975

can be reduced to combinations of two signs: you and I. The rest of the pronouns are obstacles or stimuli, walls or doors. The relationship between I and you is the copulative or adversative conjunction. The world is an analogy of the primordial pair and its changes reflect those of the you and the I in their unions and separations. That you and I, generic but not impersonal, is the only personage in a great part of Cummings's poetry. It is the pair of young lovers, alone in the society of their elders but in constant communication with the world of trees, clouds, rain. The world is their talisman and they are the world's talismans. The world and the pronouns are separated by the interposing of institutions, old men's beards, old women's coifs, generals' bombs, financiers' banks, the programs of the redeemers of the human race. There is a point of convergence between lovers and the world: the poem. There, the trees embrace, the rain undresses, the girl is renewed, love is a flash of light, the bed is a ship. The poem is an emblem of the language of nature and of bodies. The heart of the emblem is the verb: the word in motion, the motor and spirit of the phrase. Conjugation of bodies, copulation of the stars: the language resolves all oppositions in the metaphoric action of the verb. The syntax is an analogy of the world and of the couple. Cummings's universe may appear to be limited; if we penetrate toward the center, it is infinite.

In 1956 Donald Allen took me to Cummings's house. He lived on a little street in Greenwich Village. The man won me with his cordiality and simplicity in the same way that the poet had won me with his shining perfection. His house was very tiny and ascetic. There were a few small pictures on the walls, painted by himself—none of them remarkable, although Cummings did not like it to be forgotten that he was also a painter. He was not very tall. Thin, his eyes clear and lively, his teeth intact, his voice grave and rich in intonations, his hair cut short. Something of a clown, a mountebank, a magician—and that sporting air of the Anglo-Americans of his generation. He was dressed simply. The only dissonant note was a red silk tie, which he showed me happily. It was his birthday, and his wife had given it to him that morning. She was slender, with pale skin, black hair, a large mouth, and that airy solidity that Yankee women have, the daughters of Artemis: a beautiful woman and a beautiful skeleton. We drank tea and spent the afternoon chatting.

Cummings told me that as a young man he had traveled through Spain in the company of John Dos Passos. They were more excited by the villages and people than by the cities and monuments. He told me that, in spite of not knowing either our language or our literature, he had been much impressed by some of the Spanish writers of the time. Dos Passos carried on long conversations with them and

> *meanwhile I studied them: by turns they terrified me and made me laugh. It didn't matter that I couldn't understand what they were saying: I was satisfied with their physical presence, their gestures, the sound of their voices.*

The shining of their eyes, the darkness of their beards, the rapture or reserve in their gestures, their silences, their interjections: Unamuno, Valle-Inclán, Jiménez, Baroja, Gómez de la Serna? I could not be sure, and I doubt if he remembered accurately. But this sympathy was genuine. Those men seemed to him a spiritual landscape.

> *They were made of the same substance as the soil and air of Spain. That was something I missed in Paris and London. And, of course, in my own country. The degeneration of the human animal is even greater here: look what they've done with Pound.*

He hated the spirit of systems, hence his antipathy toward the Communists. He was no less hostile toward the economic monopolies and political parties of his native land. He also disliked the universities and the poet-professors (a contempt he shared with William Carlos Williams, another solitary rebel, less furious and perhaps more profound than Cummings). In those days Washington and its bureaucracy exasperated him:

> *When are they going to free Pound? If Ezra is a war criminal, then so were Roosevelt and Truman. If he's crazy, he's no more so than our representatives and senators. At least he isn't mentally retarded like the man who governs us.*[1]

1. Dwight D. Eisenhower.

In his rebellion against the values of New England, where he was born, it was not difficult to hear an echo of the individualism of his Puritan ancestors. We are condemned to rebel against our fathers and thus to imitate them. It was quite late when we said good-by.

I saw him on other occasions, each time I stopped off in New York. He sent me some of his books and we corresponded for a while. It occurred to me that one of his pieces might be put on the stage in Mexico. He was enthusiastic about the idea, but just at that time our small theatrical group—Poesía en Voz Alta [Poetry out loud]—broke up. The last time I saw him, a year before his death, he showed me some photographs his wife had taken: the houses of a cave-dwelling people on a mountain in I forget what country: "Don't they look like the skyscrapers of New York?" He laughed happily. "And my countrymen are so pleased with their progress. We haven't invented a thing." I told him that skyscrapers and those caves looked alike in the photograph but not in reality. He would not believe me: "But they're the same, the same." I told him I was living in Paris. He nodded: "I'd like to go back—though not especially. I'd rather go to Greece, where my daughter lives. I'd also like to go to Mexico. Your country is truly a country." I wanted to interrupt him. "No," he said, "I know what you're going to tell me. It's better that you aren't making progress." I said: "On the contrary, Mexico has taken a great leap." He shrugged his shoulders: "Well, as long as you don't imitate us. . . . The young poets in the United States? I don't believe in drugs as a system of poetic illumination. Poetry is made with a cool head and a blazing heart—or whatever other organ. Besides, they're repeating what we did twenty years ago. They haven't gone beyond Pound or Williams or what I've written myself." We drank tea again. The conversation turned to Europe and to whether life was less expensive on a Greek island or in a Mexican village. The lights came on in the little street. I have forgotten the rest.

I have met a number of Anglo-American poets and artists. None of them has given me that sense of extreme simplicity and refinement, humor and passion, grace and daring—except the musician John Cage. But Cage is more intelligent and more complicated: a Yankee who might also be Erik Satie and an Oriental sage. Dadaism and Basho. Cummings's humor is similar to boxing (which was a gentlemen's game at one time); Cage's is less direct and more corrosive. I hardly know what to think about his music (can one think about music?); on the other hand, I know that he is one of the few poets—despite the fact that he does not write poems—in the United States today. A strange country: it has given the world some of the great poets of the nineteenth and twentieth centuries, and all of them, with the exception of Whitman, have sought an interior or exterior exile—Poe and Dickinson, Pound and Eliot, Cummings and Williams. It can be said that the same thing has happened in all of the countries in the western world: it is a characteristic phenomenon of modern times. That is true—except that the Anglo-Americans are more modern.

Cummings, lover and circus performer, also engineer and gardener of words, was profoundly Anglo-American, especially in his rebelliousness. In general, we think of the United States as the land of great things: buildings, prosperity, cataclysms, machines. There is an Anglo-American tendency toward superlatives that, though it expresses that people's immense energy, is sometimes only a grandiloquent gesture. Not even their best writers escape from the temptation to be heavyweight champions: Whitman, Pound, Faulkner, Melville (and now their painters: Pollock). There are also exceptions. One of them was Dickinson. Cummings was another. His violence, his eroticism, and even his sentimentality have a measure: the poem. The best things he wrote were small compositions that remind us, on the one hand, of Elizabethan lyrics and, on the other, of certain French poets: of Apollinaire and, even more, of Max Jacob. It is not an influence: it is a resemblance. The surprising thing in Cummings is not the passion but rather the lustrous form in which it is expressed. All of his artifices—almost always happy ones— were so many dikes and filters whose purpose was to channel and purify the verbal material. The result was a song of incomparable translucence. Cummings walked

> . . . *through dooms of love*
> *through sames of am through haves of give*
> *singing each morning out of each night*

L.K.

A Modern Hymn

[PARIS, 1961]

In 1909, while still an adolescent, Saint-John Perse wrote his first known poem: *Images à Crusoe* [Pictures for Crusoe]; in 1959 he published *Chronique* [Chronicle], his most recent poem. A half century separates these two works. Separates or unites? Both. Little remains of the world of Perse's youth. Entire societies have disappeared, others have arisen, and those that have withstood the gale have been altered to such a degree that no one could say they are the same.

Something more than time has passed during these fifty years. Certainly it is not the first period in which cataclysms have occurred. Formerly, however, the creation and destruction of empires scarcely ruffled the daily lives of men united by work and by rite to the rhythmic cycle of nature. Real life was not historical. Even up to the past century the separation between private life and public event persisted; except in rare and isolated moments—the Revolution of 1848, the Commune—history touched Baudelaire, Rimbaud, and Mallarmé only marginally. Today history not only occupies all terrestrial space—there are no longer virgin peoples or virgin lands—it also invades our thoughts, depopulates our secret dreams, pulls us from our homes, and hurls us into the public vacuum. Modern man has discovered that life in history is an errant life. Saint-John Perse knows it better than anyone. But what history separates, poetry unites.

If we reread Perse's books, we will observe that the same verbal current flows without interruption from *Eloges* [Praises] to *Chronique*. His language reabsorbs facts, transmutes them, and, one might say, redeems them. Everything that has happened during these fifty years, not excepting the poet's personal adventure, resolves into one work. Discord, breach, exile, love and love affairs, astonishment, the destruction and birth of cities, the debilitation of language, and the intolerable fever of the western sky are the images and rhymes of one vast poem. The disperseness of our world is revealed finally as a living unity. Not the

1975 RMoser

unity of a system, which excludes contradiction and is always only a partial vision, but the unity of the poetic image. It has been said that the historian is a prophet in reverse, a diviner of the past; one might add that the poet is a historian who imagines what is happening. And what is most surprising is that his images are more genuine than are so-called historical documents. If one wishes to know what really occurred in the first half of the twentieth century, one should refer, rather than to the dubious testimony of newspapers, to a few poetic works. One of them, the work of Saint-John Perse.

Images à Crusoe ends with a sentence that is, simultaneously, an evocation and a prophecy: "You awaited the moment of departure, the rising of the great wind that would at one stroke, like the onslaught of the typhoon, dislodge you, parting the clouds before your expectant eyes . . ." Thus the first strophe of *Chronique* echoes the last strophe of the book of his youth: "Great epoch, behold us: the cool of evening on the heights, the breath of open spaces on every threshold, and our brows bared to greater vistas . . ." Perse attends the rendezvous he made with himself when he was twenty years old. Age is not resignation: the world is still open and the poet's preferred image is still that of the open road. Age is not a chair beside the fire, but a night outdoors. *Chronique* is one strophe more of the poem, a reiteration of the initial theme and augury of another adventure. Another? The same adventure, always the same, always different. Every book by Perse is one strophe of a single poem, and each of these great strophes is an isolated poem. Unity and multiplicity.

What is the theme of this poem, what story do those strophes called *Eloges, Anabase* [Anabasis], *Exil* [Exile], *Vents* [Winds], *Amers* [Seamarks], and *Chronique* tell us? The work begins as a song: praise of the natural world and the first age of man. Sea, sky, and land seen through the grave and astonished eyes of a child. Praise and farewell to infancy, to its "generous fable," and to the richness of its fare. The first book, the first strophe, is the announcement of a voyage: "All the world's roads eat from my hand." It was a single step from *Eloges* to *Anabase*. Perse took that step without nostalgia, decided from that time forward to be the alien: there is no road back, no return to the native land. *Anabase* is an account of the peregrinations and movements—in space, in time, and in the closed-off precinct of sleep—of races and civilizations, a celebration of the founding of laws and cities, an evocation of great traveler birds: "Fertile land of dream! Who speaks of building?" After *Anabase* the destiny of the alien is mixed with that of the rains, the snows, and the winds, images of change and migration, powerful condensations of the word "exile." The story of our times, yes, but at the same time the account of an exile that is endless because all human history is a history of exile. The planet itself is an errant body.

Perse's adventure is precisely the opposite of circumnavigation. Every stop is a point of departure, a brief rest before continuing the journey. The geometric figure that governs this universe is the spiral, not the circle. Perse's poetry must be read as an exercise in spiritual intrepidity. His poems do not offer us shelter against the night or against the storm: they are an encampment in the open. Nothing of roots: wings. His theme is multiple and simple: all times, and time. History without characters because the only real character in history is a nameless, faceless being, half-flesh and half-dream: the man each of us is and is not. A voyage without navigational charts or compass, because the cities, the ports, the islands—all that dazzling geography—fade away the moment we touch them. Chronicle of tempests and fair breezes, annals of the wind, book of seas and rivers, stone of heaven on which one can read, as if on a stele, the signs of good and bad years. Perse's poetry unfolds beyond the bounds of optimism and pessimism, indifferent to the clash of names and the sordid litigations of morality and meanings. His morality is something different, something different his enthusiasm and his terrible energy. Perse's theme is time, our substance. Poetry of time, that buries us and banishes us. If we are anything, we are a metaphor of time. An errant image.

Annals, chronicle, voyage: epic. Except that we are confronting a singular epic poem. Its form, the only one, perhaps, that an epoch like ours could tolerate, is far from traditional. (I will add, in passing, that our century has proposed for itself the recovery of the epic genre. Even the novel, almost entirely dominated by the spirit of analysis, today is abandoning psychology, and its most daring expressions are once again moving toward poetry, with its unitarian vision and its re-creation of language.) Once the difficulties that every poem offers to unattentive eyes have been overcome, the first thing that surprises the reader of *Anabase* or *Vents* is the absence of a narrative. The poet speaks of emigrations, conquests, voyages, rites, the invention of techniques, discoveries of new lands, elections of dignitaries, councils, usurpations, celebrations, and still one cannot introduce a lineal narrative into all this disconcerting fluctuation of centuries and events. We are at the center of the whirlwind. History is movement, but we are ignorant of the direction of that movement. Perhaps the historians know? In lieu of the always provisional explanations of philosophers of history, the poet gives us the feeling and meaning of historical life. *Meaning* is not the direction of events (something, furthermore, that no one knows): the meaning of history is not beyond, in the past or in the future, but in the here and now. On this earth and in this instant man is constructing cities, founding monarchies, celebrating assemblies, drawing up codes of law; he is writing poems or preparing his destruction. In a word, he is struggling against death, making of each of his hours a work or an act: monument and ruin. Although Perse's poetry does not adopt the lineal form of narration, its subject matter is epic. With an abundance of examples that is testimony to a very rich and vital experience, he unfolds before our eyes the variety, at once admirable and laughable, of man's works, occupations, and acts. Without referring to philosophies, he brings us face to face with the immediate meaning of history: create or perish.

If the narrative disappears, dissolved in the whirlwind of movement, what happens to heroes? They all display masks. None has a name: the alien, the regent, the usurper, tragic women, the clerk, viceroys, the financier, the astrologer . . . Functions, honors, positions—some as ancient as civilization, others imaginary. Men of all classes and all classes of men. As in the work of Joyce, all the characters blend into one. And that one never speaks in his own voice. As soon as he breaks the silence he manifests himself as a multiplicity of voices and changing presences. Dialogue or monologue? At times, a choral poem; at other times, the recitation, meditation, or supplication of a single voice. Woman is women and women are the sea. The alien is the poet and the poet is language. Wind, clouds, rocks, sea—omnipotent and omnipresent in Perse's spirit—great trees, metals, the three kingdoms (and the others) are also characters. The poet is the chronicler of the rains, the historian of the snows. The annals of history blend into physical phenomena. The storm, lightning, summer are part of the gest. Or is it the reverse? Does Perse conceive of history as a natural event? Perhaps it is neither. The vision is total. History and nature are dimensions of being, extremes of the same adventure. And man? Man, too, is adventure, a wager that life has made with itself. In *Chronique* we find this strange sentence that sheds some light upon what we may perhaps call the "transhumanism" of Perse: "Engendered of no one, can we really know toward what species we advance?" The center of the poem is man, but man seen as a transitory being, one moving toward another state: "We are shepherds of the future . . ."

Classifications are dangerous. Perse's poetry does not so much resemble the traditional epic poems as the sacred books of the Orient or the Mayan cosmogonies. Along with these religious texts one would have to mention books of history, not those of historians, but those of doers: Bernal Díaz, Babur. On the other hand, Perse's work gathers together and amplifies the modern tradition, especially that following Claudel and Segalen. This tradition is born of Mallarmé and his concept of the page as animated space. In the works of these three poets, that space is blended with a vision of the great plains of central Asia. In our poet we find, in addition, another, no less powerful, terrestrial element. Frequently one forgets that, if there is a Tartar Saint-John Perse, there is also a Saint-John Perse of the American tropics and sea: the world of *Eloges* is the world of the Antilles. In this work the great plains of the Asiatic nomads and the sparkling islands of the Caribbean come together. The importance of geography, real or imaginary, to the inspiration of this French poet reveals to us once again that his picture of history is not that of our scholarly manuals or that of our philosophers; Perse's idea of the future is that of space to be encompassed or conquered: it is not a point at which one must arrive but a place that must be peopled. Space is erotic: "Young women! and a country's nature is scented with them . . ." *Amers* contains one of the great love poems of modern French poetry. And the *Récitation à l'éloge d'une reine* [Recitation in praise of a queen] and . . . but why recall other poems? Enumerations are boring. History, geography, images of the voyage and of eroticism, Perse's poetry culminates in a song to the act of singing. Word that does not exalt any specific action, rather, the original act, the pure act, word of creative energy. Why should it be surprising that it be converted into praise of man's loftiest act: the poem? A celebration of language, Perse's poetry is a return to the origins of the poem: the hymn. An exclamation to life, an approbation of existence, praise. Poetry that ignores the gods but bathes in their fountain: "Truly I dwell in the throat of a god." Our terrible epoch is not solely doubt and negation. A poet accepts it in its totality. No true poet is Manichaean. Good and evil, the dark and the luminous sides, are not separate entities, they are the two sides of a Being that is eternally *the same*—although it is never the same. The poet ignores dispute: his song is praise.

M.S.P.

Antonio Machado

[P A R I S , 1 9 5 1]

Prose and poetry, life and work, blend together naturally in the figure of Antonio Machado. His song is also thought; his thought, a reflection of the song about itself. Through poetry, Machado moves outside himself, seizes time and the forms within which time unfolds: a landscape, the beloved, a lemon tree standing before a white wall. Through thought he recovers himself, conceives himself. Poetry and reflection are vital operations. But it is not his life that sustains his work. Rather, the reverse is true: the life of Machado the gloomy Segovian professor, the absent-minded recluse, is supported by the work of Machado the poet and philosopher. In the same way that his first poems may be understood completely only in the light of his last meditations, his life is intelligible only through his work. It is his work's creation. And his death's. His life acquired its full significance through his death; or, to be more precise, when he died—two days after having crossed the French frontier with the remnants of the Popular Army—his life was finally realized, consummated. Previously his life had been all dream and reflection: dreaming, or dreaming that he dreamed, aspiring to realize himself through something beyond himself, but something through whose contact he could become himself. Machado always said that he had not been present at the most important event of his life, although he had recalled it many times in dreams. That was the afternoon his parents first met and fell in love. I am sure that when he died he did something more than recall that encounter: the lovers on that afternoon of sun and sea and sailboats along the banks of the Guadalquivir truly began to exist.

One must not confuse naturalness with simplicity. No one is more natural than Machado, and nothing is more elusive than that naturalness. His poetry is as clear as water. As clear as running water and, like water, as impossible to grasp. The masks—Abel Martín, Juan de

Mairena—with which the poet covered his face, so that the philosopher Machado may speak with greater freedom, are transparent. Machado disappears behind that transparency. He slips away because of "fidelity to his own mask." Abel Martín, the Sevillian metaphysician, and Juan de Mairena, the professor of gymnastics and rhetoric, the inventor of a poetry machine, are and are not Machado the poet, the philosopher, the French professor, the Jacobin, the lover, the recluse. The mask, identical to his face, is elusive. Each time it is surrendered, it smiles: something has still not been expressed. To understand the erotic metaphysics of Abel Martín, we must attend to the comments of Juan de Mairena. These lead us to Machado's poems. Every personage carries us to another. Every fragment echoes, alludes to, and emblematizes a secret totality. That is why it is not possible to study only a portion of his work. It must be embraced as a whole. Or, more accurately, one must embrace each of its parts as a totality, since each is a reflection of that hidden unity.

Although Machado's work is indivisible, it does have different strata. Each stratum is seen through the transparency of another. Machado's clarity is dizzying. To read him is to sink, to penetrate into an unending transparency: into a consciousness that reflects itself. Machado's masks seem to tell us that they are something more than masks: they are the changing forms in which a perpetually mobile face has become fixed. Elusiveness is a provocation, and its only object is that of exciting our thirst. Machado, that self-absorbed man, knows that he can reveal himself only in "otherness," in an opposite that is a complement: the poet in the philosopher, the lover in absence, the recluse in the crowd, the prisoner of the "I" in the "thou" of the beloved or in the "we" of people.

Abel Martín interrogates his creator: he wants to know who was this poet Antonio Machado and what did his poems mean. Perhaps, he insinuates, nothing radically different from what his prose expresses or what, with greater clarity and conciseness, his life and his death affirm: the I, the consciousness of self, is a way of life peculiar to modern man. It is his fundamental condition: to it he owes all that he is. But it is a condition that asphyxiates him and ends by mutilating him. In order to be, in order for the I to be realized and achieve its fullness, change is necessary: the I aspires to thouness, oneness to otherness; "to be is to covet being what one is not." But reason persists in remaining identical to itself and reduces the world to its own image. By affirming itself it denies objectivity. Abel Martín rejects as illusion all forms in which comprehension apprehends objectivity, because in each of them the object is reduced to the tyranny of subjectivity. Only in love is it possible to capture what is radically "other" without reducing it to consciousness. The erotic object—"that opposes the loved one like a magnet, attracting and repelling"—is not a representation but a true presence: "Woman is the obverse of being." As he apprehends the irreducible erotic object—the phrase is not contradictory because only to reason is the object ungraspable—the lover touches the frontiers of true objectivity, he transcends himself, he becomes other. Machado is the poet of love, his mask, the philosopher Abel Martín, tells us.

In Machado's poems love appears almost always as nostalgia or remembrance. The poet is still imprisoned in subjectivity: "The beloved does not appear at the rendezvous, the beloved is absence." Machado's metaphysical eroticism has in it nothing of Platonism. His women are not archetypes but creatures of flesh and blood; however, their reality is phantasmal; they are empty presences. And his lover is Onan or Don Juan, the two poles of solitary love. Beloved and lover coincide only in absence, both trapped in a temporality that hurls them beyond themselves and at the same time isolates them. Absence is the purest form of temporality. Erotic dialogue is transformed into monologue, that of lost love, of dreamed love. The poet is alone with time, confronting time. Machado's poetry is not a song of love, it is a song of time. Machado is the poet of time, the critic Juan de Mairena tells us.

As poet of time, Machado aspires to the creation of a temporal language that will be living word within time. He disdains baroque art because it kills time by attempting to enclose it in conceptual prisons. He wants to possess it alive, as did Bécquer and Velázquez, those "jailers of time." The poetry of time will be that poetry farthest removed from conceptual language; it will be concrete, fluid, common, ordinary language: popular speech. His love for the language of the people blends with his love for traditional poetry: Jorge Manrique and the old Spanish ballads. Machado's traditionalism is the opposite of what one would call a cult of the past; rather, it is a cult of the present, of that which is always present. He is a traditional poet because the people are the only living tradition of Spain. The rest—church, aristocracy, military: the past—is an empty structure that, through its very pretension to atemporality, oppresses and mutilates the living present, popular and traditional Spain.

Granted, the language of time perhaps is not the spoken language of Castile's ancient cities. At least, it is not the language of our time. Those are not our words. The idiom of the large modern city, as Apollinaire and Eliot understood it, is something different. Machado reacted to the rhetoric of Rubén Darío by returning to tradition; but other adventures, and not a return to the old ballads, awaited Spanish-language poetry. Years later Huidobro, Vallejo, Neruda, and other Spanish American poets sought and found the new language: the language of our time. It was not possible to follow Machado and Unamuno in their return to traditional forms, and that is the reason for their negligible influence on the new poets. Something similar may be said about the Hispanicism of some of Machado's poems (in the slightly oppressive and unbreathable meaning that the word has for us Spanish Americans). It is here that elusiveness appears more clearly and becomes ambivalence. Because Machado—unlike Juan Ramón Jiménez—was the first to foresee the death of Symbolist poetry; furthermore, he was the only one among his contemporaries and immediate successors who was aware of the situation of the poet in the modern world. At the same time, he closed his eyes to the adventure of modern art. This adventure, as we all know, consists above all in discovering the poetry of the city, in transmuting the language of the urban area, not in regressing to the idiom of traditional poetry. Machado understood our situation but his poetry does not express that understanding. In this sense his prose is more fecund than his poetry.

Time escapes him. In order to recapture it, in order to revive it, he will have to *think* it. The poet of time is also its philosopher. Reflection about time leads him to thoughts about death. Man is projected into time: all life is projection into a time whose only perspective is death. Machado confronts death, but he does not perceive it, in the manner of

the Stoics, as something radically different from life or, in the manner
of the Christians, as transit or the leap from this world to the other.
Death is a part of life. Life and death are two halves of the same sphere.
Man realizes himself in death. Only, contrary to what Rilke believed,
death, for the Spanish poet, is not the realization of the I; *the I is unrealizable*. Imprisoned in subjectivity, imprisoned in time, man realizes
himself when he transcends himself: *when he becomes other*. We find
our realization in death when, far from dying our own deaths, we die
with others, in the place of others, and for the sake of others. In one of
the last texts we have by Machado, written shortly before the fall of
Barcelona, the poet tells us that the hero, the common soldier, the Spanish militiaman, "is the only one who realizes that freedom for death of
which Heidegger speaks." And he adds: "The sudden disappearance of
the young gentleman [*señorito*] and the no less sudden appearance
of gentlemanliness [*señorío*] in the faces of the militiamen are two con-
comitant phenomena. Because death is a matter for men, and only a
man—never a *señorito*—can look at death face to face." In order to die
for others you must live for others, affirm unto death the life of others.
Machado, at the end of his life, denies the enemies of the Spanish people
any possibility of transcending themselves, of giving life to others with
their deaths. These men are condemned to dying badly, to dying alone.
Their death is sterile.

Meditation on death is thus converted into a new reflection on what
Machado himself called "the essential heterogeneity of being." Being is
pure eroticism, thirst for otherness; man realizes himself in woman, the
I in the community. The most personal poetry will be that which expresses the most universal and common vision. Machado realizes that
there is a contradiction between his song and his thought. And thus he
justifies his personal lyric: the modern poet sings to himself because he
does not encounter themes of communion. We are living the end of a
world and of a style of thinking: the end of bourgeois lyricism, the end
of the Cartesian I. At the frontiers of love and death, enclosed in his
solitude, the poet sings the song of time: he counts the hours remaining
until all masks fall and man, freed at last from himself, can be reconciled with man. Only the people—"the late-born son of the exhausted

bourgeoisie"—through the revolutionary transformation of the human condition, will be able to break the shell of subjectivity, the rock crystal prison of the Cartesian I. The erotic metaphysics of Abel Martín, the anguish of time suffered by Juan de Mairena, the solitude of Antonio Machado, all flow into history.

Machado possessed intuitive insight into the essential themes of the poetry and philosophy of our time. His vision of being as *heterogeneity and otherness* seems to me to touch the very heart, the central theme, of contemporary philosophy; his lack of confidence in the Hegelian dialectic—source of so many of the evils of our era—and his insistence on examining the principle of identity through new eyes also show, and with great profundity, that the critique that philosophy makes of itself and of its fundamentals coincides with the loftiest aspirations of poetry. Novalis thought that "superior logic would abolish the principle of contradiction." Machado's work offers a way to attain that future logic. Furthermore, no one among us has lived with greater lucidity the conflict of the modern poet exiled from society and, finally, exiled from himself, lost in the labyrinth of his own consciousness. The poet does not find himself because he has lost everyone else. We have all lost our common voice, the human and concrete objectivity of our fellow beings. Our poet valorously lived this contradiction. He always refused the transcendency offered by belief in a God-Creator. For Machado, the divinity is man's creature (God is the author of the "great Zero" and his only creation is Nothingness). Blasphemous and reticent, passionate and skeptical, Machado rejects everything—except man. But his point of departure—and herein reside his great originality and the fecundity of his work—is not consciousness of the self but of its absence, nostalgia for the thou. This thou is not the generic objectivity of a faithful member of a party or of a church. The poet's thou is an individual, irreducible being. Concrete metaphysics, a metaphysics of love and—let us say the word—of *charity*.

Through the process of a dialectic of love, Machado's man finds himself only when he surrenders himself. There is a moment when the thou of love is converted into the we. In 1936, by the light of burning churches, the poet could contemplate for the first time the appearance

of that *we* in which all contradictions are resolved. Beneath the purify-
ing flames, the face of the Spanish people was the same as that of love or
death. Liberty had become incarnate. Abel Martín, Juan de Mairena,
and Antonio Machado were not alone. They had ceased to be masks:
they were beginning to be. They could die: they had lived.

M.S.P.

Jorge Guillén

[DELHI, 1965]

Jorge Guillén occupies a central place in modern Spanish poetry. It is central in a paradoxical way: his work is an island, yet at the same time it is the bridge uniting the survivors of Modernism and the Generation of '98 to the Generation of 1925. His three great predecessors, who conceived of the poem as meditation (Unamuno), exclamation (Jiménez), or word in time (Machado), surely looked upon the appearance of his first works as heresy. Machado, at least, spoke out. In an article in 1929, after welcoming "the recent admirable books of Jorge Guillén and Pedro Salinas," he added:

> These poets—perhaps Guillén more than Salinas—tend to leap like bullfighters into that central zone of our psyche where the lyric has always been born. . . . They are richer in concepts than in intuitions. . . . They give us, in each image, the last link of a chain of concepts. . . . This artificially hermetic lyric is a baroque form of the old bourgeois art.

Some years later, in 1931, he reiterated:

> I feel I am out of tune with today's poets. They propose the detemporalization of the lyric . . . especially by employing images more in a conceptual than an emotive function. . . . The intellect has never sung, that is not its mission.

In other articles I have concerned myself with Machado's ideas on poetry, so here I will repeat only that his criticism of modern poets is part of his repudiation of the baroque aesthetic. Aside from the fact that his condemnation of the baroque is unjust, it is a confusion to identify it

NOTE: Apropos of the publication of *Cántico: A Selection*, ed. Norman Thomas di Giovanni (Boston: Atlantic Monthly Press–Little, Brown & Co., 1965).

with modern art. Both the baroque and the modern poet believe that the metaphor—the image or conceit—is the center of the poem; its function is to create surprise, the "marvel that suspends the soul," through the discovery of unsuspected relationships among objects. However, the modern image is an acceleration of the relationships among things and it tends always to be dynamic and temporal, whereas the baroque conceit and metaphor are congealed movement. The poetry of our seventeenth century aspires to enthrall: its goal is beauty. Modern poetry is an explosion or an exploration: destruction or discovery of reality. The first is an aesthetic; the second, a religion, an act of faith or of desperation. The baroque poem is a verbal monument: a classicism that contemplates itself and, in so doing, re-creates itself. The modern poem is an emblem, a conjugation of signs: a romanticism that reflects upon itself and destroys itself. In sum, the baroque poem is the reflection of a Renaissance construction, distorted by the changing waters of the river or the mirror; the modern poem perches at the edge of the abyss: its foundation is criticism and its subject matter the discontinuous current of the consciousness.

When I compare them to the tendencies of the avant-garde, Guillén's poems also seem to be something akin to a silent scandal. Silent because of their reserve; scandal because of their apparent negation of time. (Again, time.) Like Unamuno, Machado, and Jiménez, the vanguardists emphasized the identification between word and "elapsing," only in a more radical and more lucid way. To submit oneself to the "inexhaustible murmuring" of the Surrealist inspiration; to give oneself to the suicidal act of Dadaistic absurdity (today repeated ad nauseam by talentless disciples who have converted its practice into a secure routine); to believe, as Huidobro believed, that the image is solely flight, thus confusing creation and release—these were and are simply various ways to dissolve the word in time. And what of the *ultraístas?* Argentine and Spanish *ultraísmo* had no aesthetic—it had a great poet, Jorge Luis Borges, also obsessed by time, although not time as elapsing but as repetition, or cessation of movement: eternal return, or eternity. Thus, what separates Jorge Guillén from his predecessors is what unites him with his contemporaries: the image; and he is differentiated from them by his concept of the poem. For the Surrealists and Dadaists, what is important is the poetic experience, not the poem. For *creacionismo*, poetry is reduced to the verbal object: the poem. In the prologue to the North American selection, *Cántico* [Song], Guillén defines in a sentence the purpose that animated him: "It was essential to identify—to the ultimate—poem and poetry." He believed that time in a poem is neither nature's time (if nature has time) nor human time. Because it is a sign, the word is a notation of elapsing, a notation that itself elapses and changes. These notations, words that are rhythms and rhythms that are words, in their distinct associations and oppositions engender another time: a poem, in which, while always hearing the flow of human hours, we hear *other* hours. The hours Fray Luis de León heard in the silence of the serene night. One could say that Guillén's poems are like music: "A mechanism to kill time." I prefer, notwithstanding, a longer and more accurate formula: a mechanism that kills time in order to revive it in other time. A mechanism of symbols, itself a symbol of the world that is created every day before our eyes.

Guillén's attitude toward language was less theoretical and more direct than that of his predecessors and contemporaries. He did not ask himself what language is but what words are and how one should group them to elicit that strange entity one calls a poem. A selection and composition of phrases and terms, the poem is a conjugation of signs fixed on the page; at the moment they are read they acquire life, they shine or they are extinguished: they signify. The poem: a mechanism of significances and rhythms that the reader sets in motion. It is astonishing that in Spain and Latin America he has been criticized as an intellectual poet. In truth, the only intellectual poets of this epoch were two Spanish Americans: the Mexican José Gorostiza and the Argentine Jorge Luis Borges. Because they are intellectuals they are poets *of* time —they are not *in* time, as Machado wished. (We are all in time, we all are time, but only a few ask themselves what happens when time passes: they are true poets of time. Borges and Gorostiza belong to the great tradition of intellectual poetry: Coleridge, Leopardi, Valéry . . .) Although we can extract a doctrine from Guillén's work—Jaime Gil de Biedma has done it ably—the Castilian poet did not propose to meditate but to sing. Meditation is not in his song: it sustains it. He is the least intellectual poet of his generation, by which I do not mean that he is the least intelligent. Perhaps just the opposite: he exercises his intelligence in his poems, not outside them. Like all intelligence, his is critical; like all creative criticism, it is invisible: it is not in what he says but in how he says it and above all in what he does not say. Silence is a part of language and an authentic poet is distinguished more by the temper of his silences than by the sonority of his words. Guillén's intelligence is not speculative; it is knowledge in action, a sentient wisdom; a feeling for weight and heat, the color and meaning of words, not excluding the almost incorporeal monosyllable.

Artisan's intelligence at the service of the act: a form of instinct. Except that this is a lucid instinct capable of reflecting upon itself. For that reason it is also consciousness. It is not strange that Guillén has been compared to Valéry. Although his first poems reveal a reading of the French poet, the resemblance is superficial: by this I mean that it is a similarity of appearances or surfaces, not of coloration, intonation, or meaning. In both poets the word tends to be transparent, but the physical and spiritual realities we see through that transparency are very different. Valéry's clarity is an act of a consciousness that contemplates itself to the point of obliterating itself. The words do not reflect the world; those breasts and serpents, those isles and columns that appear in Valéry's poems are a landscape of sensitive signs, fictions the consciousness invents in order to prove to itself that it exists. The theme of "La jeune parque" [The young Fate] is consciousness of self; and, if the theme of *Le cimetière marin* [The graveyard by the sea] is not the nonexistence of self, it is about its unreality: the I is condemned to thinking about itself without ever touching the flaming surface of the sea. "The more I think about you, Life, the less you surrender yourself to thought." Consciousness lives from what it kills, "secretly armed with its nothingness." Valéry's dialogue is with himself; *Cántico* is "the dialogue between man and creation." Guillén's transparency reflects the world, and his word is perpetual will for embodiment. Seldom has the Castilian language achieved such corporeal and spiritual plenitude. Totality of the word. Guillén has been called the poet of being. That is precise, on the condition that being is conceived of, not as idea or essence, but as presence. In *Cántico* being actually *appears*. It is the world, the reality of this world. Multiple and unique presence, a thousand adorable or terrible appearances resolved into one powerful affirmation of pleasure. Joy is power, not dominion. It is the great Yes with which being celebrates itself and sings of itself.

Guillén's word is not suspended above the abyss. It knows the intoxication of enthusiasm, not the vertigo of the void. The earth that sustains his word is this earth we tread every day, "prodigious, not magical"; a marvel that physics explains in a formula and the poet welcomes with an exclamation. To have his feet firmly on the ground is a reality that enraptures the poet; I will say, moreover, that flight also exhilarates him, for the same reason: the leap is no less real than gravity. He is not a realistic poet; his theme is reality. A reality that custom, lack of imagination, or fear (nothing frightens us so much as reality) prevents us from seeing; when we do see it, its abundance alternately fascinates and annihilates us. *Abundance*, Guillén underlines, not beauty. Abundance of being: things are what they are and for that reason they are exemplary. On the other hand, man is not what he is. Guillén knows that, and thus *Cántico* is not a hymn to man: it is the praise man makes to the world, praise from the being who knows he is nothing to the being filled with being. The cloud, the girl, the poplar, the automobile, the horse—all are presences that enchant him. They are the gifts of being, the gifts life gives us. Poet of presence, Guillén sings of the present: "The past and the future are ideas. Only the present is real." The now in which all presences unfold is a point of convergence; the unity of being is dispersed in time; its dispersion is concentrated in the instant. The present is the point of view of unity, the instantaneous clarity that reveals it. *Cántico* is a sentient ontology . . . But I am reducing many intuitions, moments of awe, exclamations to ideas and concepts, and I am thus disfiguring certain quotidian and singular experiences. Uplifted by the great vital wave, the poet exclaims: "To sing, to sing without design." Without design, not without measure. Joy bursts forth from rhythmic abundance; joy, in turn, is rhythmic. Onomatopoeia and refrain adjust to measure and acquire significance: "Mármara, mar, maramar . . ."[1] To sing without design, not without beat or meaning.

1. This play on the basic word *mar* ("sea"), in addition to its pleasant rhythm, suggests various other words, among them *múrmura* ("murmur"),

Exaltation of the world and of the instant has caused various critics to point out a certain affinity between the Spanish poet and Whitman. Guillén himself has emphasized more than once his kinship to the author of *Leaves of Grass*. The resemblance is deceptive. Whitman sees being more as movement than as presence. The contemplation of movement, which in other spirits produces vertigo (nothing remains; creation and destruction, yesterday and tomorrow, good and evil are synonymous), is converted in the work of the North American poet into celebration of the future. His reality is the future: not what we see but what is to come. Behind Guillén lies the old Hispanic-Catholic notion of substance; behind Whitman, the vision of becoming. And more: the idea of the world as action; reality is what I make it. For that reason Whitman is a poet naturally at home in history—especially if one believes, as he believed, that history means people in movement. Whitman's true landscape is not nature but history: what men make of time, not what time makes of us. Following *Cántico* Guillén wrote another book: *Clamor*.[2] Its theme is the "negative elements: evil, disorder, death." Satire, elegy, morality: the poet facing contemporary history. The differences leap into view. For Guillén history is evil; for Whitman it is the irresistible movement of cosmic life that is, in this time and in this place, embodied in the exploits of a people destined for universality. The Castilian poet is *facing toward* what happens and for that reason he writes satires and elegies, forms that imply distance and judgment; the North American *becomes* a part of the ascendant movement of history —he is history itself and his song is a celebration, not a judgment, of what is happening.

Clamor shows another aspect of Guillén the man and thus reveals to us the exactitude of Camus's phrase "solitary: solidarity." But I fear that this book does not reveal another aspect of his poetry. Guillén is not Whitman. Neither is he Mayakovsky. This is not surprising: to Span-

---

miramar ("sea view"), and several combinations of *mar* and *amar* ("to love").—*Trans.*

2. *Clamor* consists of three volumes: *Maremágnum* [Confusion], *Que van a dar en la mar* [Rivers that flow to the sea], and *A la altura de las circunstancias* [Abreast of circumstances].

iards and Latin Americans history is not what we have done or what we do, rather it is what we have allowed others to do to us. For more than three centuries our way of living history has been to suffer it. Like the majority of the Spaniards of his generation, Guillén suffered it: war, oppression, exile. Nevertheless, history is not his passion, although it is his right and honest preoccupation. If there *is* a poet in the Spanish language for whom history has been both choice and destiny, shared and apportioned passion, that poet is César Vallejo. The Peruvian does not judge. Like Whitman, he participates, although in the inverse sense. He is not the actor, he is the victim. In this way, he is also history. Guillén's theme is more vast and more universal than Vallejo's, but it is also more external: he denounces evil, he does not expiate it. Evil is not only what is done to us but also what we ourselves do. To recognize that is to encounter one of the few routes of access to true history; that was the great achievement of *The Fall*, an exemplary book. (It is good to say it now that it has become fashionable to underrate Camus's works.) I want to be understood: when I say that Guillén does not interiorize evil, that he does not make it his own, and therefore that he does not conjure it or exorcise it, I am not reproaching his moral attitude or accusing him of Manichaeism. The lowering of tension in many passages of *Clamor* simply confirms that a poet's universality—and Guillén is a universal poet—does not depend upon the extent of his moral, philosophical, or aesthetic preoccupations but upon the concentration of his poetic vision. Some are called to write *Cántico* or *Anabase* [Anabasis], others *The Pisan Cantos* or *Poemas humanos* [Human poems].

Guillén's influence on the poetry of our language has been profound and fertile. Profound, because it has been the opposite of a style—the choice of a few isolated poets; fertile, because it was a critical example and thus taught us that all expression implies silence and all creation, criticism. He was a master from the first, as much for his contemporaries as for those of us who came later. Federico García Lorca was the first to recognize it; I am sure I shall not be the last. His elders also realized the significance of his poetry, and Machado's criticism is streaked with conscious admiration. I refer to Machado because in my judgment he is the antipode of Guillén—something, actually, that Machado knew better than anyone. Two poets I admire attacked him ferociously. We often see smallness in the great among us: must one recall Quevedo, Góngora, Lope de Vega, Mira de Amescua? (I mention the dead because I prefer not to remind myself of some no less illustrious among the living.) But Guillén is a great poet because of the perfection of his creations, not because of the influence he exercised. His poems are true poems: verbal objects closed upon themselves, animated by a cordial and spiritual force. That force is called enthusiasm. Its other name: inspiration. And something more: fidelity, faith in the world and in the word. The world of the word as much as the word of the world: *Cántico*. Confronting the spectacle of the universe—not the spectacle of history—Guillén once said: *The world is well made . . .* Confronting his work, one need only repeat those words.

M.S.P.

III.

Poetry of Solitude and Poetry of Communion and A Literature of Foundations

Poetry of Solitude
and Poetry of Communion

[MEXICO CITY, 1942]

Reality—everything we are, everything that envelops us, that sustains and, simultaneously, devours and nourishes us—is richer and more changeable, more alive, than all the ideas and systems that attempt to encompass it. In the process of reducing nature's rich, almost offensive spontaneity to the rigidity of our ideas, we mutilate its most fascinating element: its naturalness. Man, as he confronts reality, subjugates it, mutilates it, and submits it to an order that belongs, not to nature (if by chance nature possesses anything equivalent to what we call order), but to thought. Thus we do not truly know reality, but only the part of it we are able to reduce to language and concepts. What we call knowledge is knowing enough about a thing to be able to dominate it and subdue it.

I do not mean, of course, that technique is knowledge. But, even when it is not possible to extract a technique (that is, a procedure for transforming reality) from knowledge, all processes of learning are still the expression of an anxiety to have this untouchable reality in our power —on our own terms and for our own ends. It is no exaggeration to call this human attitude a desire for domination. Like a warrior, man struggles to subdue nature and reality. His instinct for power is expressed not only in war, in politics, in technics but also in science and philosophy, in everything that has come to be called, hypocritically, disinterested knowledge.

This is not the only attitude that man may assume when faced with

NOTE: This paper was read at a series of lectures organized by the Séneca publishing house to commemorate the fourth centenary of the birth of Saint John of the Cross.

the world's reality and his own consciousness. His contemplation may have no practical consequence, and thus he may derive no knowledge, no opinion, no salvation or condemnation from it. This impractical, superfluous, and unserviceable contemplation is not directed toward learning, toward the possession of what is contemplated; it intends only to immerse itself in its object. The man meditating in this fashion does not propose to learn anything; he wants only to forget himself, to prostrate himself before what he sees, to become a part, if possible, of what he loves. His astonishment in the presence of reality leads him to deify it; fascination and horror move him to become one with his object. Perhaps the root of this attitude of adoration is love, which is an instinct to possess the object; a desiring, but also a fervent wish for fusion, for forgetfulness, and for dissolution of the self in "otherness." In love we find not only the instinct that impels us to survive or to reproduce ourselves: the instinct for death, the true instinct for perdition, the soul's force of gravity, is also a part of its contradictory nature. Silent rapture, vertigo, the seduction of the abyss, the desire to fall, infinitely and without rest, each time deeper, are nourished in love; also nostalgia for our origin, man's obscure movement toward his roots, toward his own birth. Because in love the couple attempts to participate once again in that state in which death and life, necessity and satisfaction, dream and act, word and image, time and space, fruit and lip blend together into a single reality. The lovers descend toward always more ancient and naked states: they recover the animal and even the plant that live in each of us; and they experience a presentiment of the pure energy that moves the universe and the inertia into which the vertigo of that energy is transformed.

The innumerable and varied postures man assumes when facing reality may be reduced—with all the dangers of such excessive simplification—to these two attitudes. Both are found with a certain purity in the magic and religion of archaic societies (although, strictly speaking, magic and religion are inseparable, since there are religious elements in all magic activity, and vice versa). Whereas the priest prostrates himself before his god, the magician rises up against reality and, convoking the occult powers, bewitching nature, compels the rebellious forces to obedience. One supplicates and loves, the other coaxes and coerces. So, is the poetic process a magic or a religious activity? Neither. Poetry cannot be reduced to any other experience. But the spirit that expresses it, the means it employs, its origin and its end may well be magic or religious. In the case of the sacred, the attitude crystallizes into plea, into prayer, and its most intense and profound manifestation is the mystic ecstasy: the surrender to the absolute, and union with God. Religion— in this sense—is dialogue, loving relationship with the Creator. The lyric poet also undertakes a dialogue with the world; there are two extremes in this dialogue: one, solitude; the other, communion. The poet always attempts to communicate, to unite (*reunite* would be more accurate) with his object: his own soul, the beloved, God, nature . . . Poetry leads the poet toward the unknown. And lyric poetry, which begins as an intimate bedazzlement, ends either in communion or in blasphemy. It does not matter whether the poet makes use of the magic of words, of the bewitchment of language, to woo his object: he never intends to utilize it like the magician, but rather to become one with it like the mystic.

In the fiesta or in the religious performance man attempts to change his nature, to strip himself of his own and to participate in that of the divine. The Mass is a liturgy, a mystery in which the dialogue between man and his Creator culminates in communion, as well as an actualization or representation of the Passion of Jesus Christ. If by virtue of baptism the sons of Adam acquire the liberty that allows them to make the leap between their natural state and the state of grace, through communion Christians are able, in the shadows of an ineffable mystery, to eat of the flesh and drink of the blood of their God. That is, they may nourish themselves with a divine substance, with *the* divine substance. The sacred feast deifies the Aztec the same as the Christian. This appetite is no different from the lover's or the poet's. Novalis said: "Perhaps sexual desire is simply desire disguised as human flesh." This thought of the German poet, who sees in woman "the most elevated corporeal nourishment," illumines for us the character of poetry and love: we try to recapture our paradisiacal nature through the medium of ritual cannibalism.

It is not strange that poetry has provoked suspicious—when not scandalized—reactions among those souls who saw pulsating within it the same appetite and the same thirst that move the religious man. In contrast to religion, which exists only when it is socialized in a church, in a community of the faithful, poetry is manifested only when it is individualized, when it is embodied in a poet. Its relation to the absolute is private and personal. Religion and poetry both tend toward communion; both begin in solitude and attempt, through the means of sacred nourishment, to break that solitude and return to man his innocence. But whereas religion is profoundly conservative, sanctifying the social bond as it converts society into church, poetry breaks that bond as it consecrates an individual relation that is marginal to, if not opposed to, society. Poetry is always dissident. It needs neither theology nor clergy. It attempts neither to save man nor to build the city of God: its intent is to give us the terrestrial testimony of an experience. As an answer to the same questions and needs that religion satisfies, poetry seems to me to be a secret form—illegal, irregular—of religion: a heterodoxy, not because it does not admit dogma, but because it manifests itself in a private and many times anarchical way. In other words, religion is always social—except when it is transformed into mysticism —while poetry, at least in our era, is individual.

What is the testimony of the poetic word, strange testimony to the unity of man and world, to their original and lost identity? First of all, it is testimony to the innate innocence of man, as religion is testimony to his lost innocence. If the one affirms sin, the other denies it. The poet reveals man's innocence. But the poet's testimony is valid only if it succeeds in transforming experience into expression, that is, words. And not just any words or words in any order whatever, but words in an order that is not thought, or conversation, or prayer. An order that creates its own laws and its own reality: the poem. For that reason a French critic has been able to say that, "while the poet is inclined to the word, the mystic is inclined to silence." This difference in aims is what ultimately distinguishes the mystic experience from poetic expression. Mysticism is immersion in the absolute: poetry is expression of the absolute or of the lacerating attempt to arrive at it. To what does the poet aspire when he expresses his experience? Poetry, Rimbaud said, desires to change life. It does not attempt to embellish it, as aesthetes and literati believe, or make it more just or good, as moralists dream.

Through the word, through expression of his experience, the poet endeavors to make the world sacred; with the word he consecrates the experience of men and the relations between man and world, man and woman, man and his own consciousness. He does not attempt to beautify, hallow, or idealize what he comes in contact with; rather, he attempts to make it sacred. Therefore, poetry is neither moral nor immoral, just nor unjust, false nor true, beautiful nor ugly. It is, simply, poetry of solitude or of communion. Because poetry, testimony of ecstasy, of blessed love, is also testimony of despair. And it may be as much blasphemy as it is plea.

Modern society cannot forgive poetry its nature. To modern man poetry seems sacrilegious. And although this nature may be disguised, although it may take communion at a common altar and then justify its intoxication with all manner of excuses, social conscience will always reprove it, consider it deviation and dangerous madness. The poet tends to participate in the absolute, like the mystic, and he tends to express it, as do liturgy and the religious festival. Since the poet's activity does not benefit society, this pretension converts him into a dangerous being, a true parasite who, instead of attracting for its benefit the unknown forces that religion organizes and apportions, disperses them in a sterile and antisocial enterprise. In communion the poet discovers the world's secret force, the force that religion through ecclesiastical bureaucracy attempts to channel and utilize. And the poet not only discovers this force and immerses himself in it, he also shows it to other men in all its terrifying and violent nakedness, pulsating in the word, alive in that strange mechanism called a poem. Need one add that this force, alternately sacred and damned, is the force of ecstasy, of vertigo, that bursts forth like sorcery at the peak of carnal or spiritual contact? At the height of that contact and in the profundity of that vertigo man and woman touch the absolute, the realm where contradictions are reconciled and life and death make a covenant on lips that meet and blend together. In that instant body and soul are one and the skin is like a new consciousness, consciousness of the infinite spilled toward the infinite . . . Touch and all other senses cease to serve pleasure or knowledge, cease to be personal; they expand, one might say, and, far from serving as antennae, as instruments of consciousness, they dissolve consciousness into the absolute, reintegrate it into original energy. Force, appetite longing to exist to the limits and beyond the limits of being, hunger for eternity and space, thirst that does not retreat before the fall but instead, in its vital excess and self-laceration, seeks to explore the eternal fall that reveals immobility and death, the black kingdom of oblivion; hunger for life, yes, but also for death.

Poetry is revelation of the innocence that breathes in every man and woman, innocence we may all recapture the moment love illumines our eyes and returns to us our astonishment and fecundity. Its testimony is the revelation of an experience in which all men participate, an experience concealed by routine and everyday bitterness. Poets have been the first to reveal that eternity and the absolute are within the reach of our senses, not beyond them. This eternity and this reconciliation with the world are produced in time and within time, in our mortal lives, for neither love nor poetry offers us immortality or salvation. Nietzsche said: "Not eternal life, but eternal aliveness: that is what matters." A society like ours, counting among its victims its best poets, wanting only to preserve itself, to endure, a society in which self-preservation and economy are the only laws, a society that prefers renouncing life to exposing itself to change, must condemn poetry—that vital extravagance—when it cannot domesticate it with hypocritical praise. And it does condemn it, not in the name of life, which is adventure and change, but in the name of the mask of life, in the name of the instinct for preservation.

In certain epochs poetry has been able to coexist with society and its impulse has nourished the best undertakings of society. In primitive times poetry, religion, and society together formed a living and creative unity. The poet was magician and priest, and his word was divine. That unity was broken thousands of years ago—at that very moment when division of labor created a clergy and the first theocracies were born—but the schism between poetry and society was never total. The great divorcement began in the eighteenth century and coincided with the downfall of the beliefs that were the foundation of our civilization. Nothing has replaced Christianity, and for two centuries we have lived in a kind of spiritual interregnum. In our epoch poetry cannot live within what capitalistic society calls its ideals: the lives of Shelley,

Rimbaud, Baudelaire, and Bécquer are proofs that spare the necessity of argument. If, toward the end of the last century, Mallarmé was able to create his poetry outside of society, today all poetic activity, if it is truly poetic, must oppose that society. It is not strange that for certain sensitive souls the only possible vocation is solitude or suicide; neither is it strange that for others, beautiful and passionate, the only imaginable poetic activities are dynamite, political assassination, or the gratuitous crime. In certain cases, at least, one must have the courage to say that one sympathizes with those explosions, which are testimony of the desperation to which a social system based solely upon the conservation of the status quo, and especially economic gain, leads us.

The same vital force, lucid in the center of its darkness, moves both yesterday's and today's poets. Except that yesterday communion was possible, thanks perhaps to the same church that now impedes it. And it must be said: for the experience to be realized once again, a new kind of man will be necessary, and also a society in which inspiration and reason, rational and irrational forces, love and morality, the collective and the individual will be reconciled. This reconciliation occurs fully in Saint John of the Cross. One need not recall the nature of the saint's society; everyone knows that it was one of the last epochs of human culture when, instead of opposing each other, the contradictory forces of reason and inspiration, society and the individual, religion and individual piety complemented and harmonized with each other. In the breast of that society, when perhaps for the last time in history the flame of personal piety could be nourished from the religion of society, Saint John realized the most intense and complete of experiences: communion. A little later that communion became impossible.

We can contemplate in all their truth the two extreme notes of lyric poetry, communion and solitude, throughout the history of our poetry. There are two equally impressive texts in our language, the poems of Saint John and a poem by Quevedo, "Lágrimas de un penitente" [Tears of a penitent], until now little studied by critics. The poems of Saint John relate the most profound mystic experience in our culture. It seems unnecessary to enlarge upon their significance since they are so perfect that they preclude any attempt at poetic analysis. Naturally, I am not saying that psychological, philosophical, or stylistic analysis is not possible; I am referring to the absurd pretension that attempts to explain poetry. When it achieves the perfection of "Cántico espiritual" [Spiritual canticle], poetry explains itself. The same is not true of Quevedo's poems. In "Lágrimas de un penitente," Quevedo expresses the certitude that the poet is no longer one with his creations; he is mortally divided. Something very subtle and very powerful intrudes between poetry and the poet, between God and man: the consciousness. And what is more significant: the consciousness of that consciousness, the consciousness of *self*. Quevedo expresses this demoniac state in two lines:

> *The waters of the abyss*
> *where I became enamored of myself.*

At the beginning of the poem the poet, lucid sinner, refuses to be saved, rejects grace; he is attached to the world's beauty. Facing God, he feels alone and rejects redemption, imprisoned in external appearances:

> *Nothing undeceives me,*
> *I am bewitched by the world.*

But the sinner realizes that the world that enchants him, the world to which he is so strongly bound by love . . . does not exist. The nothingness of the world reveals itself to him as something real, so that he feels himself enamored of this nothingness. It is not, however, the empty and nonexistent beauty of the world that prevents him from transcending himself and communicating; it is his consciousness of self. This feature lends an exceptional character to Quevedo's poem in the poetic landscape of the seventeenth century; there are other more inspired, more perfect and pure poets, but this lucidity regarding self-laceration breathes in none other. One must call this lucidity Baudelairean. In effect, Quevedo says that consciousness of self is awareness that one exists in evil and nothingness, a pleasurable consciousness of evil. Thus, he attributes a sinful content to consciousness, not so much for those sins it commits in its imaginings as for its attempts to sustain itself in itself, to be sufficient unto itself alone, and alone to satiate its thirst for the absolute. While Saint John pleads with and supplicates the Loved One, Quevedo is solicited by his God. But he prefers to lose Him and lose himself rather than offer Him the only sacrifice He will accept: his consciousness. At the end of the poem a need for expiation, consisting of the mortification of the "I," surges forth: only at this price is reconciliation with God possible. The account of this reconciliation gives the impression of a rhetorical or theological artifice, either because communion has not really been generated or because the poet was not able to express communion with the same intensity with which he told of his enchantment and of his funereal pleasure in knowing himself to be in the nothingness of sin, the nothingness of self. In truth, Quevedo's response is intellectual and stoic: he embraces death, not in order to recover life, but in resignation.

All poetry moves between these two poles of innocence and consciousness, solitude and communion. Modern man, incapable of innocence, born into a society that makes him naturally artificial, that has stripped him of his human substance to convert him into goods, seeks in vain the lost man, the innocent man. All of the worthwhile strivings of our culture since the end of the eighteenth century are directed toward recovering, toward dreaming, that man. Incapable of articulating the duality of consciousness and innocence in a poem (since it corresponds to irreducible antagonisms of history), we substitute for it either external, purely verbal rigor or the babbling of the unconscious. The mere participation of the unconscious in a poem turns it into a psychological document; the mere presence of thought, often empty or speculative, dehumanizes it. Academic discourses or sentimental vomit. And what is there to say of the political discourses, the harangues, the newspaper editorials that mask themselves with the face of poetry?

Nevertheless, poetry continues to be a force capable of revealing to man his dreams and of inviting him to live those dreams in the light of day. The poet expresses the dream of man and the world and tells us that we are something more than a machine or an instrument, a little more than that blood spilled to enrich the powerful or to maintain injustice in power, something more than goods and labor. At night we dream, and our destiny manifests itself, because we dream what we might be. We are that dream and we are born only to realize it. And the world—all men now suffering or rejoicing—also dreams and longs to live its dream in the light of day. Poetry, as it expresses these dreams, invites us to rebellion, to live our dreams awake: to be no longer the dreamers, but the dream itself.

In order to reveal man's dream it is essential not to renounce consciousness. What is asked of the poet is not abandon but greater discipline. We want a superior form of sincerity: authenticity. In the past century a group of poets who represent the hermetic branch of Romanticism—Novalis, Nerval, Baudelaire, Lautréamont—showed us the way. They are the outcasts of poetry, those who suffer nostalgia for a lost state in which man is one with the world and its creations. And sometimes the presentiment of a future state, an innocent age, springs from that nostalgia. They are original poets not so much—as Chesterton said—for their novelty as for their descent to origins. They did not seek novelty, that siren who disguises herself as originality; they found true originality in rigorous authenticity. In their endeavor they maintained an awareness of their delirium, and such audacity brought them a punishment that I do not hesitate to call envious. Misfortune fed on each of them in the form of madness, early death, or flight from civilization. They are the *poètes maudits*, yes, but they are something more: they are the living and mythic heroes of our time, because they embody—in their mysterious and sordid lives and in their precise and unfathomable work—all the clarity of consciousness and all the desperation of appetite. The seduction that these masters—our only possible masters—exercise upon us is due to the veracity with which they embody the proposition that attempts to unite the two parallel tendencies of the human spirit: consciousness and innocence, experience and expression, the act and the word that reveals it. Or as one of those masters said: *The Marriage of Heaven and Hell.*

M.S.P.

A Literature of Foundations

[PARIS, 1961]

I s there such a thing as Spanish American literature? Since the end of the last century it has been said that our letters are a branch from the Spanish trunk. Nothing is more true, if we are speaking only of language. Mexicans, Argentines, Cubans, Chileans—all of us Spanish Americans write in Spanish. Essentially our language is no different from that which is written in Andalusia, Castile, Aragon, or Estremadura. It is well known that there is greater linguistic unity in the Americas than in Spain. It could not be otherwise: we never experienced the Middle Ages. We were born at the dawn of modern times and the Castilian that reached our shores was a language that had already arrived at universality and maturity. If there is anything lacking in American Spanish, it is the particularities of the Middle Ages. True, we have created others, but there is no danger that the particularities of Argentine or Central American speech will give birth to distinct languages. Although Spanish is not eternal—no language is—it will last as long as the other modern languages: we live the same history as the Russians, French, or English. But the language that Spanish Americans speak is one thing and the literature they write is another. The branch has grown so much that it is now as big as the trunk. Actually, it is another tree. A different tree, with greener leaves and a more bitter sap. The birds nesting in its boughs are unknown in Spain.

Spanish American literature or literatures? If we open a book on the history of Ecuador or Argentina, we find a chapter dedicated to the nation's literature. But nationalism is not only a moral aberration; it is also an aesthetic fallacy. Nothing distinguishes the literature of Argentina from that of Uruguay, the literature of Mexico from that of Guatemala. Literature is broader than frontiers. It is true that the problems of Chile are not those of Colombia and that a Bolivian Indian has little in common with a Negro of the Antilles. But the multiplicity of situations, races, and landscapes does not deny the unity of our language and culture. Unity is not uniformity. Our literary groups, styles, and tendencies do not coincide with our political, ethnic, or geographic divisions. There are no national schools or styles; on the contrary, there are families, lineages, spiritual or aesthetic traditions, universals. Chilean poetry and the Argentine novel are geographic labels; but realism, creationism, criollismo, and the other aesthetic and intellectual tendencies are not. Our artistic movements are born in this or that country, of course; if they are genuinely fecund, they quickly leap the frontiers and put down roots in other lands. In addition, the present political geography of Latin America is deceptive. Its multiplicity of nations is the result of circumstances and calamities that are remote from the reality of our peoples. Latin America is a continent artificially dismembered by a conjunction of native oligarchies, military bosses, and foreign imperialism. If these forces disappear (and they are going to disappear), the boundaries will be different. The very existence of a Spanish American literature is one of the proofs of the historical unity of our nations.

A literature is always born facing a historical reality, often despite that reality. Spanish American literature is no exception to this rule. Its exceptional character resides in the fact that the reality against which it contends is a utopia. Our literature is the response of the real reality of Americans to the utopian reality of America. Before having our own historical existence, we began by being a European idea. We cannot be understood if it is forgotten that we are a chapter in the history of European utopias. It is not necessary to go back to More or Campanella to prove the utopian nature of America. It is enough to recall that Europe is the fruit—in some ways involuntary—of European history, whereas we are its premeditated creation. For many centuries Europeans did not know they were Europeans, and only when Europe was a historical reality did they suddenly realize it, realize that they pertained to something vaster than their native cities. And even today it is not certain that Europeans feel themselves to be Europeans: they know it, but that is very different from feeling it. In Europe, reality preceded the name. America, on the other hand, began by being an idea. A victory for nominalism: the name engendered the reality. The American continent had not yet been wholly discovered when it had already been baptized. The name they gave us condemned us to being a new world. A land choosing its future: before being, America already knew what it would be. As soon as he reached our shores the European immigrant lost his historical reality: he ceased to have a past and was changed into a projectile aimed at the future. For more than three centuries the word "American" designated a man who was defined not by what he had done but by what he would do. A person who has no past, only a future, is a person with little reality. Americans: men of little reality, men of little weight. Our name condemns us to being the historical project of a foreign consciousness: the Europeans.

From its very beginnings Anglo-Saxon America was a utopia on the go. The Spanish and Portuguese Americas were constructions outside of time. In both cases: the abrogation of the present. Eternity and the future, heaven and progress, all deny today and its reality, the humble evidence of each day's sun. And here our resemblance to the Anglo-Saxons ends. We are children of the Counter Reformation and the Spanish empire; they are children of Luther and the Industrial Revolution. Therefore they breathe easily in the rarefied atmosphere of the future. And for the same reason they are not in close touch with reality. The so-called realism of the Anglo-American is pragmatism—an operation that consists in lightening the compact materiality of things in order to change them into process. Reality ceases to be a substance and is transferred into a series of acts. Nothing is permanent because action is the favored form that reality assumes. Each act is instantaneous; in order to prolong itself it has to change, to become another act. The Spanish and Portuguese Americas were founded by a civilization that conceived of reality as a stable substance; human, political, or artistic actions had no other object than to crystallize in works. These works, as embodiments of the will for permanence, are designed to resist change. When I hear it said that Whitman is the great poet of American reality I shrug my shoulders. His reality is the desire to touch something real. Whitman's poetry is hungry for reality. And hungry for communion: it goes from no man's land to every man's land. Saxon America suffers from a hunger for being. Its pragmatism is an always unrealizable utopia and that is why it ends up as nightmare. It does not seek the reality of the senses, what the eyes see and the hands touch, but rather the multiplication of the image in the mirror of action; it changes reality but does not touch or enjoy it. The nomadism of the Anglo-Americans—a shot aimed at the future, an arrow that never reaches the target—is not spatial but temporal: the land they walk is a future land.

At the end of the nineteenth century, Spanish American literature ceased to be a reflection of Spanish literature. The Modernist poets suddenly broke with the Spanish models. But they did not turn their eyes toward their own lands; instead, they looked toward Paris. They were in search of the present. The first Spanish American poets to be aware of their own selves and their historical singularity were a generation of exiles. Those who could not get away invented Babylons and Alexandrias according to their resources and their fantasies. It was a literature of evasion and, at the same time, an attempt to fuse with modern life, to recover the present. They wanted to be up to date, to be in the universal mainstream. Our portion of the New World was an old, locked house, half convent, half barracks. The first thing to be done: knock down the walls, wake up the sleepers, clear the specters from their minds. (Those phantasms were, and are, very real: a stubborn past that would not go away unless it was rooted up by force.) If the exorcisms of the Modernist poets did not dissipate the specters, at least they let in the light. We could see the world: we were at the beginning of the twentieth century. We had to make haste. Among the exiles there were some who turned their eyes toward Spanish American reality: was there something, outside that Spanish past, at once grandiose and immobilized? Some poets, more through imagination than memory, glimpsed an immense natural world and the ruins of brilliant and cruel civilizations lost among jungles and volcanoes. The literature of evasion soon became a literature of exploration and return. The true adventure was in America.

Almost always the road to Palenque or Buenos Aires went by way of Paris. The experience of those poets and writers reveals that in order to return to our home we must first dare to abandon it. Only the prodigal son returns. To reproach Spanish American literature for its rootlessness is to ignore the fact that only this rootlessness permitted us to recover our portion of reality. Distance had to precede discovery. Distance, and also the mirages it created—it is not harmful to feed on illusions if we transform them into realities. One of our mirages was the natural world of America; another, the Indian past. Now, nature is no more than a point of view: the eyes that behold it and the will that alters it. Landscapes are poetry or history, vision or work. Our lands and cities took on a real existence as soon as our poets and novelists named them. The same thing did not occur with our Indian past. On the one hand, our Indians are not past but present—a present that breaks in on us. On the other hand, they are not nature, they are human realities. Indigenous literature in its two aspects—the ornamental and the didactic, the archaeological and the apostolic—has failed doubly, as artistic creation and as social preachment. Much the same can be said of Negro literature. There are Indian and Negro writers in Spanish America who are among our best, but they do not write *of* but *from* their condition. One of the most impressive works of our contemporary letters is an anthropological document: the autobiographical narrative of Juan Pérez Jolote, an Indian of Chiapas.

The rootlessness of Spanish American literature is not accidental; it is the consequence of our history, of our having been founded as a European idea. But, having assumed it fully, we went beyond it. When Rubén Darío wrote *Cantos de vida y esperanza* [Songs of life and hope] he was not a Spanish American writer who had discovered the modern spirit: he was a modern spirit who had discovered Spanish American reality. This is what distinguishes us from the Spaniards. Antonio Machado believed that a Spanish work could be universal only by first being profoundly Spanish; Juan Ramón Jiménez called himself "the universal Andalusian." Spanish American literature unfolds in the opposite way: we do not think that Argentine literature is universal; however, we believe that some works of universal literature are Argentine. What is more, we have discovered, thanks to our rootlessness, a buried tradition: the ancient indigenous literatures. The influence of Nahuatl poetry on various Mexican poets has been very profound, but perhaps those poets would not have recognized themselves in those texts, at once restrained and delirious, if they had not undergone the experience of Surrealism or, in the case of Rubén Bonifaz Nuño, of Latin poetry. Is it not significant that the translator of Virgil is also one of those who has best understood the "modern" qualities of indigenous poetry? And, in the same way, Neruda had to write *Tentativa del hombre infinito* [Attempt of the infinite man], a Surrealist exercise, before arriving at his *Residencia en la tierra* [Residence on earth]. What is that earth? It is American and at the same time it is Calcutta, Colombo, Rangoon. One could add many other examples: the novels of Bioy Casares and Cortázar, the poems of Lezama Lima and Cintio Vitier . . . But that is not necessary: a book by the Argentine poet Enrique Molina is entitled *Costumbres errantes o la redondez de la tierra* [Errant customs or the roundness of the earth].

A return is not a discovery. What have Spanish American writers discovered? Almost all of Borges's work—and I am thinking not only of his prose but also of many of his poems—postulates the nonexistence of America. Borges's Buenos Aires is as unreal as his Babylons and Ninevehs. Those cities are metaphors, nightmares, syllogisms. What is that metaphor saying, what is that dream dreaming? Another dream, named Borges. And *that* dream? Another. In the beginning, someone dreams; if he wakes up, the dreamed reality disappears. Under pain of death we are condemned to dream a Buenos Aires where a Borges is dreaming. This poet's works postulate not only the nonexistence of America but also the inevitability of its invention. Or to say it in another way: Spanish American literature is an enterprise of the imagination. We are resolved to invent our own reality: the light at four o'clock in the morning on a greenish wall in the outskirts of Bogotá; the vertiginous fall of darkness on the city of Santo Domingo (in a house in the center of town a revolutionary awaits the arrival of the police); the hour of high tide on the coast of Valparaíso (a girl undresses and discovers solitude and love); the cruel noonday in a village in Mexico's state of Jalisco (a farm hand has dug up a pre-Conquest sculpture; tomorrow he will go to the city; an unknown woman is awaiting him there, and a journey . . .). To invent reality or to rescue it? Both. Reality recognizes itself in the imaginings of poets—and poets recognize their imaginings in reality. Our dreams are waiting for us around the corner. Spanish

American literature, which is rootless and cosmopolitan, is both a return and a search for tradition. In searching for it, it invents it. But invention and discovery are not terms that best describe its purest creations. A desire for incarnation, a literature of foundations.

L.K.

Index

Abrojos (Darío), 33 n
"Adiós, El" (López Velarde), 100–101, 103
Alberti, Rafael, 72
Albigenses, 98
Allen, Donald, 133
Altura de las circunstancias, A la (Guillén), 158 n
Amers (Perse), 139, 142
Anabase (Perse), 139–140, 141, 159
Anderson Imbert, Enrique, 33
Apollinaire, Guillaume, 61–62, 68–69 n, 136, 148. Works: *Calligrammes*, 68 n; "Lettre-océan," 68 n
Arnim, Joachim von, 19
Art Nouveau, 23, 27, 38
Ateneo de la Juventud, 69
"Augurios" (Darío), 54
Azul (Darío), 31, 33–34

Babur, 142
"Bailarín, El" (López Velarde), 71
Balmaceda, Pedro, 33
Baroja, Pío, 134
Baroque literature, 9, 11, 13, 18, 79, 106, 147, 153–154
Basho, 60, 135
Baudelaire, Charles, 17, 20, 21, 22, 23, 33, 38, 40, 54–55, 60, 69, 70–71, 73, 105–106, 137, 169, 172. Works: "La chambre double," 71; "L'examen de minuit," 54; *Les fleurs du mal*, 37; "Le gouffre," 55; "L'horloge," 71; "Mademoiselle Bistouri," 71; "Madrigal triste,"

105–106; *Le spleen de Paris*, 71
Beardsley, Aubrey, 23
Bécquer, Gustavo, 17, 33, 147, 169
Bello, Andrés, 28
Bioy Casares, Adolfo, 178
Bloy, Léon, 22
Bonifaz Nuño, Rubén, 178
Borges, Jorge Luis, 19, 74, 122, 154, 155, 178
Byzantinism, 120

Cage, John, 135–136
Calderón de la Barca, Pedro, 7, 17, 19
Calleja, Father P. Diego, 8, 13
Calligrammes (Apollinaire), 68 n
Campanella, Tommaso, 174
"Campanero, El" (López Velarde), 101
Campoamor y Campoosorio, Ramón de, 33
Camus, Albert, 158, 159. Work: *The Fall*, 159
"Candil, El" (López Velarde), 74, 109–110
Cántico (Guillén), 155, 156–157, 158, 159, 160
"Cántico espiritual" (Saint John of the Cross), 170
"Canto a la Argentina" (Darío), 49
Canto a la Argentina y otros poemas (Darío), 41 n, 48
"Canto de esperanza" (Darío), 48, 49
Canto errante, El (Darío), 41 n
Cantos de vida y esperanza (Darío), 35, 41–42, 48, 54, 69, 177

Carta atenagórica (Sor Juana), 3–4
Casal, Julián de, 21, 23, 34
Castilian literature. *See* Spanish
  literature
Castro, Eugenio de, 22, 28
Castro, Rosalía de, 17
Cathari, 101–102, 106, 108
Cervantes, Miguel de, 17, 19–20.
  Work: *Los trabajos de Persiles y
  Segismunda*, 19–20
"Chambre double, La" (Baudelaire),
  71
Chesterton, G. K., 172
Chirico, Giorgio di, 73
"Christ's Proofs of Love for Man"
  (Vieyra), 3
Chronique (Perse), 137, 139, 142
Cimetière marin, Le (Valéry), 156
Cisnes y otros poemas, Los (Darío),
  41 n
Clamor (Guillén), 158–159
Claudel, Paul, 142
Coleridge, Samuel Taylor, 17, 155
"Coloquio de los centauros" (Darío),
  39–40
Commune, the, 137
Communist Manifesto (Marx and
  Engels), 45 n
Confucianism, 46
Conquest of Spanish America, 6, 178
Contemporáneos, 69
Contreras, Rafaela, 34–35
Coppée, François, 33
Cortázar, Julio, 178
*Costumbres errantes o la redondez
  de la tierra* (Molina), 178
Counter Reformation, 7, 175
Cranach, Lucas, 87
Creacionismo, 155

Cruz, Sor Filotea de la. *See*
  Fernández de Santa Cruz, Manuel
Cruz, Sor Juana Inés de la, 3–15, 18;
  attitude toward learning, 4, 7–8,
  11–15; dreams as a theme, 12–15;
  love as a theme, 9–11; and New
  Spain, 4–6, 7; poetic style, 6–7,
  8–9, 13; and religion, 3–4, 6–7, 11,
  12. Works: *Carta atenagórica*, 3–4;
  El divino Narciso, 7, 9; *Primero
  sueño*, 7, 8, 9, 11, 13–15; *Respuesta
  a Sor Filotea de la Cruz*, 4, 8, 9,
  12; *villancicos*, 6, 8–9
Cummings, E. E., 131–136

Dada, 60, 135, 154–155
Dante, 103, 105, 106. Work: *Divine
  Comedy*, 101, 105
Darío, Rubén (Félix Rubén García
  Sarmiento), 18–19, 21, 22–23, 26,
  29, 31–44, 47–56, 69, 148, 177;
  attitude toward Spain, 26–27,
  43–44; attitude toward United
  States, 44, 47–49; death as a theme,
  54–56; eroticism as a theme,
  38–39, 49–52, 55; and French poetry,
  31–34, 35; and Modernism, 18–19,
  21, 22–23, 26–27, 29, 31, 33, 35,
  43; occult as a theme, 52–54;
  poetic style, 33–34, 37–38, 41–43.
  Works: *Abrojos*, 33 n; "Augurios,"
  54; *Azul*, 31, 33–34; "Canto a la
  Argentina," 49; *Canto a la
  Argentina y otros poemas*, 41 n,
  48; "Canto de esperanza," 48, 49;
  El canto errante, 41 n; *Cantos de
  vida y esperanza*, 35, 41–42, 48, 54,
  69, 177; *Los cisnes y otros poemas*,
  41 n; "Coloquio de los centauros,"

39–40; "Ecce Homo," 33; "Epístola," 42, 48; *Epístolas y poemas*, 31, 41 n; *Prosas profanas*, mental," 55 n; "Poema del otoño," 55; *Poema del otoño y otros poemas*, 31, 41 n; *Prosas profanas*, 34, 35–40, 41, 42, 43; *Los raros*, 22, 35; "Refutation of President Taft," 40 n; *Rimas*, 33 n; "Salutación al águila," 47; "Serenata," 33; "Spes," 54; "To Roosevelt," 44, 49; "Trébol," 42; "Venus," 34
De Rougemont, Denis, 101–102
"Derrota de la palabra, La" (López Velarde), 104–105
Des Esseintes (pseud. of Darío), 36 n
Día, Un (Tablada), 60–61, 73
"Día trece" (López Velarde), 97
Díaz, Bernal, 142
Díaz, Porfirio, 63
Díaz Mirón, Salvador, 21, 24, 34, 84 n
Dickinson, Emily, 136
Díez-Canedo, Enrique, 69
Divine Comedy (Dante), 101, 105
Divino Narciso, El (Sor Juana), 7, 9
Don de febrero, El (López Velarde), 67, 97
Dos Passos, John, 134
Dostoevsky, Feodor, 76, 121

"Ecce Homo" (Darío), 33
Eliot, T. S., 74, 136, 148. Work: "The Love Song of J. Alfred Prufrock," 74
Eloges (Perse), 137, 139, 142
Emerson, Ralph Waldo, 44
Engels, Friedrich, 25. Work:

Communist Manifesto, 45 n
"Epístola" (Darío), 42, 48
Epístolas y poemas (Darío), 33 n
Euripides, 117, 118
"Examen de minuit, L' " (Baudelaire), 54
Exil (Perse), 139

Fall, The (Camus), 159
Faulkner, William, 136
Feria, La (Tablada), 63, 64
Fernández de Santa Cruz, Manuel, 3–4
Fin de Satan, La (Hugo), 20
Fleurs du mal, Les (Baudelaire), 37
Fortún, Fernando, 69
Frost, Robert, 125–130
Fuensanta, 81, 84–88, 93, 94, 100–101, 103–104, 105, 108, 110
Fuentes de Fuensanta (Noyola Vázquez), 98 n

García Lorca, Federico, 19, 72, 159
García Sarmiento, Félix Rubén. *See* Darío, Rubén
Gautier, Théophile, 21, 33
Gavidia, Francisco, 32
Generation of 1925, 153
Generation of '98, 153
George, Stefan, 22
Gil de Biedma, Jaime, 155
Goethe, Johann Wolfgang von, 23, 117, 118
Gómez de la Serna, Ramón, 74, 134
Góngora, Luis de, 9, 13, 17, 72–73, 79–80, 118, 120, 160. Works: "Hermana Marica," 79–80; *Soledades*, 13
Gongoristic poetry, 10, 13

González de Mendoza, José M.,
68–69 n
González Martínez, Enrique, 59, 84 n
Gorostiza, José, 75, 84 n, 155. Work:
Muerte sin fin, 76
"Gouffre, Le" (Baudelaire), 55
Gourmont, Remy de, 22
Greco, El, 15
Guillén, Jorge, 19, 153–160. Works:
A la altura de las circunstancias,
158 n; *Cántico*, 155, 156–157, 158,
159, 160; *Clamor*, 158–159;
Maremágnum, 158 n; *Que van a
dar en la mar*, 158 n
Gutiérrez Nájera, Manuel, 21, 34

Haiku, 28, 60–61
Heidegger, Martin, 149
Henríquez Ureña, Max, 34, 36 n
Henríquez Ureña, Pedro, 28
Herder, Johann Gottfried von, 72
Heredia, José María, 21, 34
"Hermana Marica" (Góngora),
79–80
Hispanism. *See* Spanish literature
Hölderlin, Friedrich, 17
"Horloge, L' " (Baudelaire), 71
"Hormigas" (López Velarde), 74
Hugh Selwyn Mauberley (Pound),
74
Hugo, Victor, 20, 31, 32–33. Work:
La fin de Satan, 20
Huidobro, Vicente, 73, 148, 154
"Humildemente" (López Velarde),
79
Hundred Years' War, 46
Huysmans, Joris Karl, 23, 36 n.
Work: *A rebours*, 23

"Idilio salvaje" (Othón), 84 n
Ifigenia cruel (Reyes), 76, 116–120
Ignatius, Saint, 7
Images à Crusoe (Perse), 137, 139
Imagist poetry, 61–62
"Insomnia" (Tablada), 61

Jacob, Max, 136
Jacobins, 25, 80, 146
Jaeger, Werner Wilhelm, 116
Jaimes Freyre, Ricardo, 27–28, 35
Jammes, Francis, 69
Jarro de flores, El (Tablada), 60–61
Jena group, 19
"Jeune parque, La" (Valéry), 118,
156
Jiménez, Juan Ramón, 17, 19, 28, 41,
55, 72, 75, 134, 148, 153, 154, 177
John of the Cross, Saint, 17, 163,
169–170. Work: "Cántico
espiritual," 170
"José de Arimatea" (López Velarde),
71
Joyce, James, 121
Juan Pérez Jolote (Ricardo Pozas),
177

Kafka, Franz, 121
Kostrowitzky, Albert, 68–69 n

Laclos, Pierre Choderlos de, 17
Laforgue, Jules, 22, 71–73
"Lágrimas de un penitente"
(Quevedo), 169–170
Lautréamont, Comte de, 22, 172
Lawrence, D. H., 121
Leaves of Grass (Whitman), 37, 158
Leconte de Lisle, Charles, 34
León, Fray Luis de, 155

Leopardi, Giacomo, 17, 155
"Lettre-océan" (Apollinaire), 68 n
Lezama Lima, José, 178
Li-Po (Tablada), 61–62
Lope de Vega Carpio, Félix, 160
López Velarde, Ramón, 19, 59, 63, 67–112; death as a theme, 91–92, 95–96, 99–101; and French writers, 70–73, 74–75; love and eroticism as a theme, 84–95, 102–106, 108–109; and religion, 96–102. Works: "El adiós," 100–101, 103; "El bailarín," 71; "El campanero," 101; "El candil," 74, 109–110; "La derrota de la palabra," 104–105; "Día trece," 97; *El don de febrero*, 67, 97; "Hormigas," 74; "Humildemente," 79; "José de Arimatea," 71; "El mendigo," 74; *El minutero*, 67, 71, 76, 87, 108; "Obra maestra," 71, 107–108; "El perro de San Roque," 77–78; "El retorno maléfico," 79; *La sangre devota*, 67, 69, 84, 87, 108; "A Sara," 87; *El son del corazón*, 67, 84, 108, 110–111; *La suave patria*, 81–83; "El sueño de los guantes negros," 86–87, 100–101, 102–103; "Tierra mojada," 74; "Todo," 74, 111; "La última odalisca," 74, 91–92, 97–98, 99; *Zozobra*, 67, 69, 84, 87, 97, 98, 108, 110–111
"Love Song of J. Alfred Prufrock, The" (Eliot), 74
Lugones, Leopoldo, 18–19, 24, 35, 71, 72–73, 93; wife of, 42, 48. Work: *Lunario sentimental*, 35, 73
Lunario sentimental (Lugones), 35, 73

Lustra (Pound), 74
Luther, Martin, 175

Machado, Antonio, 18, 28, 41, 72, 73, 130, 145–151, 153, 154, 155, 159, 177
"Mademoiselle Bistouri" (Baudelaire), 71
Madero, Francisco, 116
"Madrigal triste" (Baudelaire), 105–106
Madriz, José, 40 n
Maeterlinck, Maurice, 69
Mallarmé, Stéphane, 20, 21, 34, 35, 36, 40, 118, 121, 137, 142, 169. Works: "Hérodiade," 118; "Prose pour des Esseintes," 36 n
Mancera, Marquesa de, 8, 10–11
Manichaeism, 45, 47, 98, 101–102, 105, 143, 159
Manrique, Jorge, 147
Maremágnum (Guillén), 158 n
Martí, José, 21, 22, 24, 35
Marx, Karl, 45, 76. Work: *Communist Manifesto*, 45 n
Marxism, 23–24
Mayakovsky, Vladimir, 158
Mazdean tradition, 102
Melville, Herman, 136
Mendès, Catulle, 21, 33, 34
"Mendigo, El" (López Velarde), 74
Middle Ages, 98
Minutero, El (López Velarde), 67, 71, 76, 87, 108
Mira de Amescua, Antonio, 160
Modernism, 18–31, 33–35, 44, 46, 59, 60, 62, 75, 78, 118, 153, 176
Molina, Enrique, 178. Work:

*Costumbres errantes o la redondez
de la tierra*, 178
More, Sir Thomas, 174
Moréas, Jean, 35
Moreau, Gustave, 23
Morgan, Lewis Henry, 25
Muerte sin fin (Gorostiza), 76
Murillo, Rosario, 32, 33, 34–35, 56

Nación, La, 40
Nahuatl poetry, 6, 177
Neruda, Pablo, 51, 69, 74, 148, 178.
Works: *Residencia en la tierra*,
178; *Tentativa del hombre
infinito*, 178
Nerval, Gérard de, 20, 40, 87, 105,
172
Nervo, Amado, 41, 53
Nietzsche, Friedrich, 21, 22, 76, 168
Noche Triste, the, 126
Novalis, 20, 50, 105, 120, 150, 165,
172
Novo, Salvador, 84 n. Work: *Nuevo
amor*, 84 n
Noyola Vázquez, Luis, 68, 98 n.
Work: *Fuentes de Fuensanta*, 98 n
Nuevo amor (Novo), 84 n
Nuño, Rubén Bonifaz. *See* Bonifaz
Nuño, Rubén

"Obra maestra" (López Velarde), 71,
107–108
Orphism, 43, 53
Ortiz de Montellano, Bernardo, 71
"O terremoto mental" (Darío), 55 n
Othón, Manuel José, 84 n. Work:
"Idilio salvaje," 84 n
Owen, Gilberto, 84 n

Palma, J. J., 34
Paredes, Condesa de, 10
Parnassianism, 21, 32, 35
Péguy, Charles, 57
Pellicer, Carlos, 64, 84 n
Pérez Jolote, Juan. *See Juan Pérez
Jolote*
"Perro de San Roque, El" (López
Velarde), 77–78
Perse, Saint-John, 137–143. Works:
Amers, 139, 142; *Anabase*,
139–140, 141, 159; *Chronique*, 137,
139, 142; *Eloges*, 137, 139, 142;
Exil, 139; *Images à Crusoe*, 137,
139; *Récitation à l'éloge d'une
reine*, 142; *Vents*, 139, 141
Petrarch, 106
Phillips, Allen W., 67, 68–71, 73,
76, 93, 97, 109
Pisan Cantos, The (Pound), 159
Platonism, 9, 37, 49–50, 51, 147
Poe, Edgar Allan, 22, 23, 28, 31, 44,
136
"Poema del otoño" (Darío), 55
Poema del otoño y otros poemas
(Darío), 31, 41 n
Poemas humanos (Vallejo), 159
Poesía en Voz Alta, 135
Pollock, Jackson, 136
Polo de Medina, Jacinto, 6
Pope, Alexander, 17
Pound, Ezra, 74, 134, 135, 136.
Works: *Hugh Selwyn Mauberley*,
74; *Lustra*, 74; *Pisan Cantos, The*,
159
Prada, Manuel González, 24, 27
Prescott, William Hickling, 126
Primero sueño (Sor Juana), 7, 8, 9,
11, 13–15

Prosas profanas (Darío), 34, 35–40, 41, 42, 43
"Prose pour des Esseintes" (Mallarmé), 36 n
Provençal literature, 28, 49, 51, 98, 101–103, 104, 105, 106
Pythagoras, 53
Pythagorean numbers, 37

Que van a dar en la mar (Guillén), 158 n
Quevedo, Francisco Gómez de, 17, 100, 103, 105, 160, 169–171. Work: "Lágrimas de un penitente," 169–170

Ramón López Velarde: El poeta y el prosista (Phillips), 67 n, 68–70
Raros, Los (Darío), 22, 35
Rebolledo, Efrén, 69
Rebours, A (Huysmans), 23
Récitation à l'éloge d'une reine (Perse), 142
"Refutation of President Taft" (Darío), 40 n
Renaissance, 51, 98
Residencia en la tierra (Neruda), 178
Respuesta a Sor Filotea de la Cruz (Sor Juana), 4, 8, 9, 12
"Retablo" (Tablada), 63
"Retorno maléfico, El" (López Velarde), 79
Revista Azul, 21
Revolution of 1848, 137
Revueltas, Silvestre, 82
Reyes, Alfonso, 113–122. Work: *Ifigenia cruel*, 116–120
Reyes, Bernardo, 116

Richter, Jean Paul, 19–20. Work: *Titan*, 19–20
Rilke, Rainer Maria, 149
Rimas (Darío), 33 n
Rimbaud, Arthur, 22, 120, 137, 166, 169
Rodenbach, Georges, 69
Rodó, José Enrique, 44
Romanticism, 19–20, 28–29, 30, 32, 39, 51; English, 19, 20; French, 20–21; German, 13, 19, 20, 72, 76, 106, 121; Spanish, 19–20, 32, 33; Spanish American, 19, 32
Rougemont, Denis de. *See* De Rougemont, Denis
Rousseau, Henri (Le Douanier), 82
Rousseau, Jean Jacques, 17, 25
Rudel, Jaufré, 105
Ruelas, Julio, 89

Sade, Marquis de, 22, 90
Salinas, Pedro, 153
"Salutación al águila" (Darío), 47
Sánchez, Francisca, 40–41
Sangre devota, La (López Velarde), 67, 69, 84, 87, 108
Santos Chocano, José, 24
"Sara, A" (López Velarde), 87
Satie, Erik, 135
"Serenata" (Darío), 33
Shelley, Percy Bysshe, 19, 168–169
Silva, José Asunción, 21
Soledades (Góngora), 13
Son del corazón, El (López Velarde), 67, 84, 108, 110–111
Spanish literature, 17–18, 20, 22, 26–30, 43–44, 51, 69, 72, 74, 147–148, 156, 173, 176, 177
"Spes" (Darío), 54

Spleen de Paris, Le (Baudelaire), 71

Stoics, 90, 149

Story of O, The (Réage), 90

Suave patria, La (López Velarde), 81–83

"Sueño de los guantes negros, El" (López Velarde), 86–87, 100–101, 102–103

Sufism, 102

Surrealism, 30, 154–155, 177–178

Swift, Jonathan, 17

Swinburne, Algernon Charles, 22

Symbolism, 21, 29, 32, 39, 51, 60, 148; Belgian, 22; French, 29, 106

Tablada, José Juan, 28, 57–65, 68–69, 73, 84 n., 87, 97. Works: *Un día,* 60–61, 73; *La feria,* 63–64; "Insomnia," 61; *El jarro de flores,* 60–61; *Li-Po,* 61–62; "Retablo," 63

Tamerlane, 23

Tantrism, 51

Taoism, 46, 51

Tentativa del hombre infinito (Neruda), 178

Theresa, Saint, 7

"Tierra mojada" (López Velarde), 74

Titan (Richter), 19–20

"Todo" (López Velarde), 74, 111

"To Roosevelt" (Darío), 44, 49

Trabajos de Persiles y Segismunda, Los (Cervantes), 19–20

"Trébol" (Darío), 42

"Ultima odalisca, La" (López Velarde), 74, 91–92, 97–98, 99

Ultraísmo, 154

Unamuno, Miguel de, 18, 54, 134, 148, 153, 154

Uranga, Emilio, 109

Valencia, Guillermo, 24

Valéry, Paul, 155, 156. Works: *Le cimetière marin,* 156; "La jeune parque," 118, 156

Valle-Inclán, Ramón del, 19, 22, 41, 134

Vallejo, César, 148, 159. Work: *Poemas humanos,* 159

Vargas Vila, José María, 24

Vasconcelos, José, 97

Velázquez, Diego, 17, 147

Vents (Perse), 139, 141

"Venus" (Darío), 34

Verhaeren, Emile, 69

Verlaine, Paul, 22, 32, 35

Vieyra, Antonio de, 3. Work: "Christ's Proofs of Love for Man," 3

Villancicos, 6, 8–9

Villaurrutia, Xavier, 68, 69, 70, 71, 76, 84 n, 96–97, 104, 109

Villiers de l'Isle-Adam, Philippe, 22

Virgil, 49, 178

Vitier, Cintio, 178

Whitman, Walt, 22, 28, 31, 34, 36, 44, 48–49, 136, 158–159, 175. Work: *Leaves of Grass,* 37, 158

Wilde, Oscar, 22

Williams, William Carlos, 134, 135, 136

Zozobra (López Velarde), 67, 69, 84, 87, 97, 98, 108, 110–111